MW00831559

ASTRONOMICAL
GRACE

ASTRONOMICAL GRACE

The Greatest Story
Never Told

ANDREW OWEN

BREAKFAST
FOR **SEVEN**

Astronomical Grace
Copyright © 2022 Andrew Owen

All rights reserved. No part of this book may be reproduced or transmitted in any form or by any means, electronic or mechanical, including photocopying, recording, or by any information storage and retrieval system, without permission in writing from the publisher.

Published by Breakfast for Seven, a division of Inprov LLC
2150 E. Continental Blvd., Southlake, TX 76092.

Scripture quotations taken from the Amplified® Bible (AMP), Copyright © 2015 by The Lockman Foundation. Used by permission. www.lockman.org

Scripture quotations are from the ESV® Bible (The Holy Bible, English Standard Version®), copyright © 2001 by Crossway, a publishing ministry of Good News Publishers. Used by permission. All rights reserved.

Scripture quotations marked (KJV) are taken from the King James Version®. Public domain.

Scripture quotations taken from the (NASB®) New American Standard Bible®, Copyright © 1960, 1971, 1977, 1995, 2020 by The Lockman Foundation. Used by permission. All rights reserved. www.lockman.org

Scripture quotations taken from the (NASB®) New American Standard Bible®, Copyright © 1960, 1971, 1977, 1995 by The Lockman Foundation. Used by permission. All rights reserved. www.lockman.org

Scripture quotations marked (NIV) are taken from the Holy Bible, New International Version®, NIV®. Copyright © 1973, 1978, 1984, 2011 by Biblica, Inc.™ Used by permission of Zondervan. All rights reserved worldwide. www.zondervan.com The "NIV" and "New International Version" are trademarks registered in the United States Patent and Trademark Office by Biblica, Inc.™

Scripture taken from the New King James Version®. Copyright © 1982 by Thomas Nelson. Used by permission. All rights reserved.

Scripture quotations marked (NLT) are taken from the Holy Bible, New Living Translation, copyright © 1996, 2004, 2015 by Tyndale House Foundation. Used by permission of Tyndale House Publishers, Inc., Carol Stream, Illinois 60188. All rights reserved.

Scripture quotations marked TPT are from The Passion Translation®. Copyright © 2017, 2018 by Passion & Fire Ministries, Inc. Used by permission. All rights reserved. ThePassionTranslation.com.

Scripture quotations marked MSG are taken from THE MESSAGE, copyright © 1993, 2002, 2018 by Eugene H. Peterson. Used by permission of NavPress, represented by Tyndale House Publishers. All rights reserved.

ISBN: 978-1-951701-13-0 — Hardback
ISBN: 978-1-951701-14-7 — eBook

Printed in the United States of America.

CONTENTS

FOREWORD

As a Christian and a pastor for the past 45 years, I'm thankful you are receiving the life-changing message in the following pages. *Astronomical Grace* will bring you a new revelation of the gift called grace. What should be known to all who believe in our Lord Jesus, isn't. What an amazing gift this insight is for those who will receive it.

We have all struggled with the thoughts and emotions of insecurity, inadequacy and fear for our future, but most of us have found little comfort that truly answers the issues of our soul. It is obvious the secular world has no healing or help for the needs of humanity, and how sad that much of our Christian teaching has not brought the answers of healing we seek. Religion has often added to the feelings of inferiority and condemnation.

Understanding God's grace is the key that unlocks the restoration and wholeness of our souls. As David wrote: *"The LORD is my shepherd; I shall not want. He makes me to lie down in green pastures; He leads me beside the still waters. He restores my soul"* (Psalm 23:1–3, NKJV).

Astronomical Grace is a message of healing and renewal that will lift you above the hurts of this world and the negatives of religion. This is not a casual devotional. Take the time to soak it up and let it work. Don't be afraid to see the 'fake news' we've all believed and get to the 'real faith' we all need. Let's get to the crown jewels of our relationship with God and not live off the crumbs that religion has tossed us.

It may be hard for some of us to admit we've believed a lie or spent years on the wrong path, but remember that with God, every day is new and our future is in Him. I am still learning, still renewing and still discovering all He has for me. God is for us, and His desire for us is only good. His grace is much more than we have known. Let's embrace it, believe it, receive it.

I'm praying with you that these pages will meet a need and lift you to a new place in Him. We don't deserve it, we can't earn it, but we can receive it. The Lord is good, much more good than many have known. Embrace the grace.

Casey Treat
Christian Faith Center, Seattle, Washington

INTRODUCTION

When you don't get what you deserve, that's mercy; when you get what you definitely don't deserve, that's grace.

Grace is one of the most common words in the Christian vocabulary, yet millions of Christians are kept in ignorance of its truth, and consequently, its vast liberating power. Perhaps it is one of the least understood attributes of God and the gospel. Never have the words of the Lord, spoken by the prophet Hosea been so pertinent, *"My people are destroyed for lack of knowledge"* (see Hosea 4:6, NASB).

There are some really important things God wants you to know, and there are some really important things God wants you to see.

And once you see something, you cannot unsee it.

Seeing grace has caused revivals, reformations and the radical transformation of the most desperate of lives. C.H. Spurgeon, writing about Mary Magdalene said, *"Grace found her a maniac and made her a minister."* [1]

For years, I would make it a practice to read the Bible through in its entirety every calendar year, using one of the many excellent reading plans that are out there. So, it would be no exaggeration to say that I have read the Bible cover to cover dozens of times. Yet, I had not seen what I am about to share with you now, even though it was hidden in plain sight.

This revelation has got me into trouble on a number of occasions. Once, when preaching in multiple services at one of the largest churches in the UK, I was stopped from preaching these things in the second service, having just preached this message in the first service. The pastors were so shocked to hear my sermon in that first service that they asked me not to preach it again, even though dozens had come to Christ and hundreds of people responded for prayer. They told me that the revelation of grace was too *dangerous* to preach.

This revelation is unfolding, but the more I see it, the more astounded I become of God's grace. There is no other word for it — ASTRONOMICAL! Just out of this world.

But regrettably, in too many places, it really is the greatest story *never* told. The gospel is thought to be preached, but so often it's a hybrid version of it. Jesus *plus* (all of Christ and some of me) which in effect reverses the good news into bad news. We never doubt God keeping His end of the gospel message, but we do very much doubt our ability to keep anything at our end. The tailspin of condemnation and inadequacy that then follows makes for a very large number of unhappy, ineffective Christians.

Thankfully, the gospel is good news; it's all God, and nothing else needed. God knew we couldn't add even the smallest thing to our own salvation, so He undertook to complete all that was necessary. That's grace.

In the 1600's a puritan preacher and writer by the name of Thomas Brooks wrote a timeless book titled *Precious Remedies Against Satan's Devices,* that book went on to encourage many well-known preachers who came after him, including C.H. Spurgeon and Dr Martyn Lloyd-Jones. Brooks wrote that there were four very important things that should be studied and never forgotten: they are, our dearest Lord Jesus Christ, the Scriptures, the vulnerability of our own hearts, and Satan's devious devices. This book in many ways is a convergence of these four points. It is my prayer that this book will contribute something to that all important conversation on grace. The message of grace you'll find in the following pages is something I truly wish I had known from the beginning of my Christian walk. Like many people, grace was in my vocabulary, but the magnitude of its truth was yet to dawn in my heart. I'm writing this book so that you can live in the truth of God's grace from this day forward.

Over the years, there have been so many *EUREKA!* grace moments for me. Let me share some of them with you, so that you can also walk with joy, freedom and hope, knowing the gospel of our Lord and Saviour Jesus Christ brings us the most amazing truth of God's astronomical grace.

1

The Greatest Story *Never* Told

The fact that the Scriptures are brim full of hustlers,
murderers, cowards, adulterers and mercenaries used
to shock me. Now it is a source of great comfort. [2]

BONO — U2

Some people say that it was Benjamin Disraeli, a former British prime minister who once said, *'Ideas rule the world.'*

Ideas are told through the narratives of movies, sung in songs in the popular charts, written into the backstory of novels and propagated by politicians all over the planet. Ideas captivate the imagination, motivate the soul and move a person to action. Ideas give a person something to live for, and for many people, something they will die for. Ideas are invisible, yet they find life in the words of men and women, young and old. Ideas are brought to life as they are told, repeated, spoken and considered.

Ideas don't just hold the high ground of political office, but ideas roll out around kitchen tables, café meetings and pub pints. Ideas create enterprise, compose music, disrupt industries and introduce wonderful benefits for humankind. Ideas imagine the unimaginable and create new worlds around us.

Ideas are not born equal, some are horrendously designed for death and destruction, some are indifferent, nothing more than a 'nice' idea, but there are some ideas that are truly revolutionary.

God had an idea, and you were in it. That's why you are here. The Lord said to the prophet Habakkuk, *"For the earth will be filled with the knowledge of the glory of the* LORD*"* (see Habakkuk 2:14, NASB). Jesus expressed that idea when He said, *". . . I will build my church; and the gates of Hades will not overpower it"* (see Matthew 16:18, NASB). John the disciple expressed that idea when he said, *"See how great a love the Father has given us, that we would be called children of God . . ."* (1 John 3:1, NASB).

We would do well to examine the ideas that we hold, for these ideas in the end will hold us.

We should discard the indifferent and fear-inducing ideas but embrace with all our might the God-glorifying, life-giving, faith-enhancing ideas, for they will truly hold you tight.

God's idea was of a people, His people, gathering and forming around the earth. All nations, all ages, all kinds, all invited. All moving under one supreme head — Jesus Christ, God's Son. Gathering not just for the now, but for a glorious, eternal, end-time purpose in the victorious Kingdom of God.

For this idea to become a reality, it would require the massive injection of a most potent factor, this factor we call grace.

Grace is both an attribute of God and an ongoing work of God. Grace is so integral to God that it is indivisible from anything He is or anything He does.

True, we don't read in the Bible a clear-cut definition, stating *God is grace,* and we do most definitely read *God is love.* (See 1 John 4:8.) But how does the love of God reach the undeserving, the faulty and the failing? How does that love reach me?

The conduit of love is grace.

We all know God can do anything — healing, saving, providing and forgiving. But lurking in the recesses of our minds and hearts is the formidable question, *Not can He, but will He?* And if He were to do it for me, *why?* Why would He possibly commit to do anything for me when I so often fail for Him?

The Answer that I didn't Expect

I had decided to preach a series in my home church on the book of Genesis, the book of beginnings. As I set out to preach and teach my way through this book, I arrived at the 27th chapter, the scene of an elaborate fraud. This was one of my grace *EUREKA!* moments.

The story goes like this:

A mother and her son hatched a plot to steal from a brother, and deceive a blind, frail and elderly father. And not just any father, he was Isaac, the son of promise. Isaac had once been laid out on a sacrificial alter and watched a knife come down towards his heart. He would have witnessed first-hand the ram caught in the thicket that saved his life, and he would have walked back down that mountain, having heard his father Abraham coin those immortal words *Jehovah Jireh* — the Lord will provide.

This Isaac was now old and ready to die, and so was setting his estate in order by handing down the birthright blessing to his eldest son Esau. This all-important act was set to happen not in a lawyer's office, but in a tent in the backside of the desert, straight after a celebration meal. Esau, the eldest twin son born to Isaac and Rebecca, who was forever the hunter-gatherer, had gone out after game to prepare his dad's favourite dish.

Meanwhile, back at the tents, Rebecca coaxed her favourite son Jacob, the youngest of the twins, to step in first, and by deception steal that which wasn't his. Jacob protested, stating the obvious, that he was in fact nothing at all like his brother, for they clearly were not identical twins.

He didn't sound the same as Esau. He didn't even 'feel' the same; In Genesis 27:11 (KJV) Jacob says, *Esau my brother is a hairy man, and I am a smooth man.* Jacob was sure to be caught out if his blind old father would run his hands over him. The Bible points out that Jacob didn't even smell like his brother, for the fresh smells of the woodlands and fields were definitely not lingering on Jacob's coats.

Fearful then that he would end up cursed instead of blessed, Jacob contested the idea. Undeterred, mother could not be stopped, a disguise was created from goat skins which were laid on Jacob's neck and arms, and then the borrowing of Esau's personal clothes succeeded in completing the disguise.

Although initially suspicious, Isaac goes through with it, and in an irreversible action proceeded to give the 'wrong' son the birthright blessings. No sooner had this occurred that Esau returns and with terrible anguish of soul, realises he's been had. His manipulative brother, along with his doting mother, had stolen his inheritance and left him with little. Esau was mad, and mad enough to kill. Esau comforts himself with the thought that soon dad will be dead, and for certain, his kid brother will quickly follow.

The home atmosphere is charged with dark clouds of heavy anger, and so Jacob is sent away to his uncle Laban for a few days, just until things calm down. What was intended to be a few days became 25 years, and Jacob never saw his mother or his father again.

Jacob runs for his life, as far and as fast as his legs would carry him. Looking over his shoulder the whole time to see if Esau was in hot pursuit. Eventually, exhausted and tired he rests and falls asleep on the desert floor, using a stone for a pillow. At the very darkest moment, in the midnight hour, God shows up and enters Jacob's world through a dream.

What a moment.

Now, if you were God, and caught up with Jacob just at that point, what would you do or what would you say to him? And if you were Jacob, what would you expect God to say to you? Jacob had just stolen his brother's inheritance and defrauded and deceived his father, Isaac.

For sure, if I was God, I would be very clear on my course of action and my choice of words. I would make myself appear as large and as fearful as possible. I would saturate and permeate the moment with my overwhelming holiness, and I would say something like, *Caught you now! Call yourself a covenant believer? You should be thoroughly ashamed of yourself. What would your grandfather Abraham say? Consequently, this will be your judgement . . .*

And if I was Jacob, I would be expecting to hear something just like that. But God says nothing of the kind, in fact, these are His exact words:

> *"Behold, I am with you and will keep you wherever you go, and will bring you back to this land; for I will not leave you until I have done what I have promised you."*
> **(GENESIS 28:15, NASB)**

Jacob's astonished reply comes:

> *"How awesome is this place! This is none other than the house of God, and this is the gate of heaven!"*
> **(GENESIS 28:17, NASB)**

Instead of pronouncing Jacob's just and deserved judgement, God tells Jacob that He is so personally for him, that He will never leave him and will make absolutely certain that every last promise given would be fulfilled. Clearly, none of which Jacob deserved.

You have to ask, *Why would God treat a man like this?* How could He be so generous, kind and gracious? Isn't this the Old

Testament? Under an old covenant? What is grace doing appearing here in such a bold outrageous fashion?

God not only showed mercy, withholding the judgement Jacob deserved, He pronounced unending blessing, allegiance and undying fidelity to a faulty failure of a man.

The emphases I had just seen in this story was not at all what I wanted to preach or expected to expound upon as I worked my way through Genesis, but it was as if many strands of my ongoing God conversations had just merged into one moment of WOW!

God treats undeserving people with unearned favour. Such is grace. Such is God. But what about me? What about you? Do we think God would do the same for us? Bless us when we least deserve it? Extend forgiveness towards our often-repeated sins? And if He would, why would He?

I think that the greatest promise God ever made to us was that He would never leave us or forsake us (Hebrews 13:5), yet many of us think He leaves every time we sin or fall short. Many Christians live lives of quiet desperation and despair, struggling and striving, trying to get on God's good side, not realising that they are already there.

There seems to be two fundamental challenges we face, and they are not unique to us; they have been faced by every Christian who has come before us. The first challenge is that we know so little of God's grace, but perhaps the biggest challenge is that Satan turns that ignorance against us like some weapon of mass destruction.

Thomas Brooks wrote in the 1600's, *"Now Satan will tempt the soul to look up, and see God angry; and to look inward, and to see conscience accusing and condemning; and to look downwards, and see hell's mouth open to receive the impenitent soul."* [3]

Back to Jacob, his account has significance for you and me. I saw something that I admit might always have been blatantly obvious to many others: God did not deal with Jacob according to his **condition**, but God dealt with Jacob according to his **position**.

Why Did God Treat Jacob Like This?

There is a hugely important reason why I think that God dealt with Jacob with such grace on that night in the backside of the desert. This wasn't God just being kind or feeling sorry for Jacob. Neither was God turning a blind eye to this major deception he plotted and connived with his mother. There really is something substantive going on here.

Now, I know many commentators talk of this account in terms of the doctrine of election: God chose Jacob and rejected Esau, and that's all there is to it, they argue. Basically, God liked the guy and wanted him on His team. In which case, where would that leave me? Where would that leave you? We could ask in light of this idea: Is God's grace available to only some people? Are we elected or rejected?

Spurgeon would say, *"There will be no doubt about His having chosen you, when you have chosen Him."* [4] And the same Spurgeon was heard to pray, *God save all the elect and elect some more.*

So, without going any further into that discussion, it's really important that we focus on the story here for a moment. This God-given gracious action with Jacob in the dark desert night was not based on any short-term impulse. And as we shall see, this story is a type, a picture, an illustration of something so significant and great that would yet come that it would open the door for all people everywhere to receive God's astronomical grace. This grace response had started in God's heart way before Jacob was even born.

Have you ever thought of this? The story tells us that Jacob had to dress up like another man to get his father's blessing. Since the laws and cultures of the day dictated that the elder brother was the rightful heir to both the birthright blessings and birthright titles, Jacob the younger of the two, had no rightful claim to it, so on his own merits, he could not come and get it. He didn't qualify. Born too late.

Isaac was blind, but he wasn't stupid, so to make the disguise convincing, Jacob was set up to feel like his brother with the hairy goat skins wrapped around his arms and neck, and even made to smell like his brother as he borrowed his brother's garments.

You see, a very important procedure had just taken place for, with and on Jacob.

Once Jacob was perceived to be the elder brother, Isaac's hands had been laid on him, the covenant blessings had been imparted to him, and God's name was now a big part of his identity. From this point forward, God would be known as the God of Abraham, Isaac and Jacob. That's exactly how it's recorded in the Bible. It never became the God of Abraham, Isaac and Esau. Such was the significance of that moment.

God did not deal with Jacob according to his natural **condition,** but dealt with him according to **his position,** his standing if you will. Once those hands of Isaac had been laid on Jacob, he would now be standing in, on and under Abraham's calling, walking in Abraham's covenant.

God dealt with Jacob accordingly, as if Abraham, the friend of God was standing right there himself.

Now, look at this . . .

Similarly, you and I were also dressed up in another man's clothing, even set up to smell like that other man to get our Father's blessing. We are told over 200 times in the New Testament that we are in Christ. We are told multiple times to 'put on Christ', and we're even told that we smell like Christ.

> *For we are to God the pleasing aroma of Christ among*
> *those who are being saved and those who are perishing.*
> **(2 CORINTHIANS 2:15, NIV)**

Isaac was blinded by age and fooled by deception, but our Father did it by design, on purpose and with His eyes wide open! Furthermore, Esau was an unwilling victim, even more faulty in character than his sly brother Jacob, but our elder brother was a complicit participator, perfect in character, faultless in nature and complete in obedience.

Jesus, whom the Bible calls our elder brother (see Hebrews 2:11, Romans 8:17), chose to participate in the identity swap.

God made him who had no sin to be sin for us, so that
in him we might become the righteousness of God.
(2 CORINTHIANS 5:21, NIV)

And that is exactly how God deals with us who are now Christians. That's exactly how grace operates. God does not deal with us according to our condition but according to our position.

For if by the offense of the one, death reigned through
the one, much more will those who receive the
abundance of grace and of the gift of righteousness
reign in life through the One, Jesus Christ.
(ROMANS 5:17, NASB)

The apostle Paul was not making a comparison in this verse, but a contrast. If sin and death have affected us all through Adam, then similarly (only much more so), the abundance of grace has come to us through this righteousness found in and from our Lord Jesus Christ.

As far as God was concerned, something very significant had happened in that moment with Isaac and Jacob, for the covenant God had made with Abraham was now activated upon and fully applied to Jacob's life. And the moment we come to Christ, the new covenant is applied to us, we are swept up in grace-filled, loving arms.

As far as God is concerned, the Christian's conversion experience is so significant and the identity swap so great, that we look and smell like Jesus before God. Spiritually speaking, we have

Jesus' DNA, retina scan and fingerprints. And we are not standing before God naked and ashamed as Adam was after he fell to sin, but we are now standing unashamed in Jesus' clothes, spotless, dressed in glorious garments of righteousness.

Just like Jacob, we didn't qualify for the Father's birthright blessings, and there was absolutely nothing that we could do to merit it.

The birthright blessing was hugely significant in Jacob's day, in that it also went part and parcel with the double portion of inheritance rights. The eldest son would inherit double, more than any other sibling. This was not simply intended to make the eldest wealthier, but resourced properly to carry out the family business, protect the family name, proclaim the name of God, and see to family worship through alters and rituals.

Important families had legacies to consider, a name to uphold, promises, hopes and dreams to be fulfilled by the next generation and the one after that. The eldest was given that lead position within the family and consequently needed to be compensated and resourced properly to make sure it happened.

Can you see what God has done in Jesus? Can you see what Grace has accomplished?

He has brought us into the birthright blessings, privileges and responsibilities. We are both fully accepted and at the same time set up to succeed.

The family inheritance rights legitimately belong to God's first Son — our Lord and Saviour Jesus Christ. He is our elder brother. But in His grace, and by His grace, He has brought us into it all! We are set up for life, not simply for our own sakes, but for His name's sake, that we might take on the kingdom family business — *God, Sons & Daughters Unlimited.*

The benefits of God's grace operate not on our ability or performance, but on our position, location and standing in Christ. This is one of the hardest aspects for any human being to see or accept — that grace is free, generous and overwhelmingly God-driven, without us paying for it, earning it or adding to it, especially when we are so often like Jacob and behave in a fashion that makes us even less deserving of anything from God.

Brought Out To Be Brought In

Hundreds of years after Jacob's story, God brought about an extraordinary victory as He led Jacob's descendants out of Egypt's tyrannical grip with great power. The ultimate aim was not to bring them out, but to take them in — into the land promised.

Similarly, God's aim is not only to bring us out of sin but to take us in to the land promised, and that isn't heaven later, it's a grace-filled life now, full of promise and power. We too are brought out so that we can be brought in.

We need to understand that we are not meant to struggle towards it but rather we learn how to stand in it. We stand in everything God has already done for us in Jesus.

Many people have been taught that God is good, but there is always a proviso added.

The proviso sounds like this: *For me to experience God's goodness in practice, I have to do better in life.*

In other words, God's activity in my life depends upon my personal performance as a believing Christian. The more *holy* or *committed* I become, then the more I can expect grace, favour and answers to prayer.

For years, I thought I believed in grace, but I was actually believing in conditional grace, which in itself is an oxymoron, a contradiction in terms. The very beauty of grace is that it is unconditional, a sheer act on God's part to the undeserving.

'God give us grace to see our need of grace; give us grace to ask for grace; give us grace to receive grace; give us grace to use the grace we have received'.

D.L. MOODY (SOVEREIGN GRACE)

2

Fake News or Real Faith?

*The only difference between being uninformed and misinformed
is that one is your choice and the other is theirs. But both
will leave you in the same place, taking as fact, fiction.*

UNKNOWN

He who controls the story, controls the world.

I heard those words from my university lecturer just a few
years ago when I had decided to return to some study and pursue a master's degree in Community Development.

His lecture was on critical theory and cultural Marxism, the
doctrine behind much of the current culture wars in our nations.

Then, recently, I heard the exact same words again, but this
time from a journalist and broadcaster who told of the seismic
shift that has happened in news reporting. She pointed out that
investigative journalism seems to have disappeared and instead

we have a new breed of reporters who are told what to write. They are frequently handed, by their editors, the *narrative* or story line that their publication will be taking.

We are not told the news, but their opinion of it, which is often a suitably slanted concoction of half-truths and polling statistics, intended to convey a very persuasive message affecting elections, public opinion and our very shaky world. The era of fake news has been born, alongside the inevitable conspiracy theory trends. Such things used to only happen in war time, and it would be called propaganda. But there is a great war, the *Holy War* as John Bunyan called it, a war for the souls of men and the conflict of kingdoms.

We all tend to believe the narrative that we are told, and too many of us as Christians have been told the wrong story concerning the truth of the gospel.

Jesus knew the power of story and was a great storyteller. Through parables and stories, He explained profound truth. Jesus' stories always caused a big reaction and a mixed response, challenging His hearers to the very core. No one was left sitting on the fence, you always went one way or another. The 'sinners' delighted in the good news it brought, and couldn't get enough, but the self-righteous Pharisees had more than enough and wanted to silence the storyteller. They realised that the stories were often about them and their legalistic, hard-as-nails, far-from-God ways. Jesus was calling them out and catching them out, whilst the whole time His heart was aching to take them out of the deadness of their desperate religion.

Many preachers and pastors have followed Jesus' example and used stories and metaphors to explain the gospel as they see it. Unfortunately, they were not as good as Jesus in the storytelling, and oftentimes the metaphors they used produced mixed messages — or worse still — mixed doctrine. With new believers not knowing much about their Bibles at the start of the Christian journey, these passionate and very sincere preachers often shaped people's theology for decades to come, passing on Christian folklore instead of Christian truth. There is an awful lot of folklore out there leaving many people carrying sincerely held beliefs that are a million miles from biblical facts and actual truth.

I'm not blaming the pastors or the preachers, since the devil is a pretty good storyteller too, and he has made sure that plenty of confusion has reached our minds and hearts as well. These hybrid versions of the gospel all too often can become core beliefs, very difficult to move and correct, and can have catastrophic consequences in the life of an individual. They often leave people with cognitive dissonance, which is a desperate state of heart and mind where the mind accepts one set of beliefs but the heart accepts another, tearing a person apart and not leaving any sense of peace, let alone the kind of peace Jesus offers.

You hear God forgives sins with your ears but receive condemnation with your heart, because you think He hasn't as yet forgiven all of your sins, especially the ones you keep repeating or the ones you forgot to confess. You hear God loves you with your ears, but believe God is out to judge you with your heart. You hear God is a God full of grace with your ears, but a holy, law giving, difficult to please Father who is never satisfied with anything less than perfection with your heart.

Demos Shakarian wrote a book called *The Happiest People on Earth*, but in my experience, all too often Christians are actually the unhappiest people on earth. My church has been broadcasting on TV across our nation several times a week for several years, which in turn gets a sizable amount of mail. The single biggest (by far) comment or request we get is, *Please pray for me. I'm just not good enough as a Christian, God cannot be pleased with me.*

The truth is this: We really should be the happiest people on earth, and the more the truth of God's astronomical grace is revealed in our lives, the more that joy unspeakable and fullness of glory is released within us. It's inevitable, unstoppable.

If My Life Story Were a Parable

Come with me on a personal journey and a walk into some profound truth. Let's determine to leave the folklore behind and remember that any time we encounter Jesus, we encounter **grace** and **truth.** Your story may not be exactly like mine, but it won't be far off, since I know the devil has played the same trick for centuries. And he may still be playing it on you.

This is how metaphors were used to explain the gospel to me, and left me insecure, unhappy, joyless and sullen. But this is also the story of how I came to a place of correcting those folklore stories and how I found the confidence that the real gospel produces — creating within me the power of an unsinkable soul. My parable went something like this . . .

I was an unworthy sinner, fallen and failing. I was told that I was standing in a filthy, dirty, sinful suit that needed cleaning up. I was only a child at the time, hardly any time at all to build up those sinful activities, but I wholeheartedly agreed with this pronouncement of judgement. I was already deeply convicted.

The good news is God loved me so much, that He sent His Son Jesus to die for me. If you come to Christ I was told, you can be born again, forgiven. You get a brand-new white suit; all your sins are washed away. And so, I came to Christ. In fact, I got saved every Sunday for many months. In each moment, I felt so clean, happy and peaceful, but by Monday, all the doubts returned and the peace vaporised. The challenge was, having gratefully received this brand-new white suit, I just couldn't keep it clean!

Condemnation was then added to my guilt and failure. I would hear, *Don't you love Him enough to keep your white suit clean?* Perhaps these words were never actually said by anyone, but certainly whispered by the devil into my heart.

Even before a Monday was over, never mind the rest of the week, something always seemed to happen which would cause a knee-jerk reaction from me that was less than saintly. In my imagination, in that moment another sinful mud pie had just landed on my clean white suit, upsetting my walk with God. Couldn't I even walk straight for one day? It was these failures followed by condemnation that would result in a weekly visit to the church altar most Sundays.

Then, the parable or the metaphor continued.

I was told, 'Listen, you don't need to get saved every week; God heard you the first time'.

Instead, I was taught how to keep my new snow-white salvation suit clean. Quoting 1 John 1:9, I was pointed in a new direction. Confess your sins, every last one of them, and look — see, it's right there in the Bible: God promises to forgive you and clean you right up.

I was grateful for this activity. There was, at last, something that I could do to remedy the situation. But I ended up in a bigger problem. Not only did I now need to confess the new and emerging sins, but I needed to go back into my past, and make sure I confessed the old ones. The resulting effect? I always worried that I had missed a few.

'Don't worry about that', I was told. 'You see, you have the Holy Spirit now, and His role in your life is to convict you of sins. He will clearly point out the things that need to be put right, and all you need to do is repeat the sequence — confess, repent, accept, move on'.

This point was further underscored with the mantra, *Keep short accounts with God, son.*

Initially, I challenged this method, pointing out some verses I had read about there being no condemnation to those who are in Christ. My teacher came right back at me, pointing out that there was a huge difference between conviction and condemnation. One, he said left you hopeless with nowhere to go (condemnation), and the other, (conviction) was a necessary step to salvation and recovery. Sounded so right, doesn't it? I didn't understand then that all of this was so far from the truth.

I took it all on board, not realising it had just tilted my relationship with the Holy Spirit. He was now to be my 'comforter' by pointing out all my errors and immature ways. I was, in effect, taught and trained like so many others to visit the spiritual dry cleaners. And like too many others, I spent a fortune of emotional money there.

I was attending a protestant church but was more diligent in confession than any Roman Catholic. The only difference was that I went directly to God instead of a human priest.

I knew Jesus had become my High Priest, and I could go directly to Him. The trouble was that I had no idea what a priest did or what my great High Priest was doing for me. I thought Jesus was just like the catholic priest; wasn't His main role to hear my sinful confession?

He might not give me five Hail Marys, but He is bound to say, *You must do better, you must try harder.*

The visit to the spiritual dry cleaners became all the more important at certain times, like just before going to church and meeting all the other 'saints', and especially before meeting the pastor, who was sure to see through me (the pressure increased if there was going to be a communion service that day). It became even more important if I needed a special prayer answered or a big favour from God like help with my exams. So, every prayer time began with a deep searching of the heart.

My prayers became more and more about repentance for sins and promises that I would make, assuring God that I would do better tomorrow. Not even thinking about some of the huge promises God had made me. I mostly stopped sharing my faith with my friends, and even when I did, I simply repeated the 'dirty sinner, dirty suit' story. In effect, I stopped praying about anything meaningful at all, not even sure about any results or effect my prayers would have. I always knew God *could* but doubted if God *would*, at least for me. I became a thoroughly miserable and unhappy person. I had the exact opposite of an unsinkable soul. I was sinking fast, trapped between loving God and wondering — how could He ever love me?

When Grace Enters the Story

Then one day, as a young teenager, the Holy Spirit took me on a personal journey. He changed the story; He rewrote the metaphor, he realigned the parable. This was one of the most profound moments in my life.

The journey began on a Thursday night when I was attending a prayer meeting at my local church, which were always powerful nights. Old timers were calling on God with passion and fire. Testimonies would flow in the weeks that followed of answered prayers and God breakthroughs.

On this particular Thursday, as I walked the three miles home in the darkness from our prayer meeting, I prayed: 'One day, Lord, I'm going to pray like these guys and get my own big, powerful answers to prayer'. I heard the Holy Spirit say right back, 'When will that day be, son?'

I was quick to respond with a Bible verse I had just heard prayed by someone that very night, 'You know, Lord, just like

James said, "It's the prayers of a *righteous* man that are power-ful and effective", 'so I guess it's when I become righteous, just like those godly old timers in that prayer meeting'. I heard the Holy Spirit again say, 'And when will you be righteous, son?' I again replied, 'I guess, Lord, when I've ironed out some of these issues between us and overcome some of the character defects in my life'.

It started right there, and I'm still not sure how long that conversation with the Holy Spirit continued. It went on for many months, but it was like a rising sun and one day it dawned on me. All the lights came on. The Holy Spirit began to change the narrative, correct the story.

When God said to me these unforgettable words, 'Andrew, you were never given a new white suit to look after; I AM YOUR WHITE SUIT! And it doesn't need looking after. It's always per-fect and pristine, and therefore, so are you in my eyes. You are in me, and so I can be in you. You are righteous already'.

This was a game changer, right then and there. I suddenly saw it — in a moment — but I've been learning more and more about it ever since. I felt like I was born again, again. I read, lis-tened, searched out anyone or anything I could find that could expand on my discovery.

Dr Martyn Lloyd-Jones, a very famous Welsh preacher who, at the time, lived in London would occasionally visit my part of Wales (a place where he himself had once lived and minis-tered). I, with many others, went and listened to him at every opportunity.

Although much of what he said went over my head in those days, he seemed so passionate about this concept of *justification by faith*. Over the years that followed, God, in his grace, took me on a journey with several amazing teachers and mentors, to all of whom I am immensely grateful.

But my best teacher has always been the Holy Spirit. He has this knack of opening up the Word for me, whilst making sure I somehow get connected to a book or a message or a person at the same time. Filling out the narrative, completing the story. And the more I see, the more overwhelmed I become by God's astronomical grace.

3

The Crown Jewels of Christianity — Justified by Faith

Therefore, having been justified by faith, we have peace with God through our Lord Jesus Christ, through whom we also have obtained our introduction by faith into this grace in which we stand; and we celebrate in the hope of the glory of God.

(ROMANS 5:1–2, NASB)

Notice that the words "having been justified by faith" are in the past tense. Paul, who wrote this epistle, is talking to Christians, and he's telling them of something that has happened for them, not something that will happen to them. Neither did he say, it is happening (i.e., a process), but he quite emphatically tells it has already taken place, and obviously whatever it is that has happened, must have happened completely.

This truth, when seen, has sparked revivals, revolutions and reformations. Justification by faith is the single biggest factor in the work of redemption. It, of course, cannot stand alone from other great aspects of our salvation, but it has to be the prized jewel in the crown. Yet too few Christians ever understand it or understand what Christ has actually done for them. And even if we see it, do we really see the magnitude of it?

The first title ever given to God in the Bible is *the judge of all the earth,* (Genesis 18:25) and all men are guilty of sin before him — no exceptions. We also read *for all have sinned and fallen short of the glory of God* (Romans 3:23). Therein lies the dilemma, how can a sinful man have a relationship with a holy God — AND BOTH ENJOY IT?

I had a relationship with God and didn't enjoy it for years and felt like God didn't enjoy it either. His perfection only seemed to shine a floodlight on my imperfections.

But the good news is that God **justifies** guilty sinners.

But what exactly does it mean to be justified?

"Justified" is a judicial term, a legal pronouncement. If a man is justified, his status or standing is altered, and permanently so. Not only is he acquitted from all charges, when justified, he is considered innocent, no case to answer. He is not like the people we watch go through trials, where those clever lawyers got them off through a technicality. No, the justified man walks away scot-free, with no inkling of a shadow hanging over his head. And since the judge passing the judgement in our case is the judge of all the earth, there is no higher court of appeal.

Furthermore, since this Judge knows all things, there is never going to be any new evidence coming to light that will call for a retrial, *it is finished* once and for all. New future sins will not alter this judgement call, they will not require a fresh assessment, no need of a new court hearing. In fact, all sins were dealt with even before we were born and before we even committed any single one of them.

In 1 Peter, we read:

> *For Christ also suffered for sins once for all time, the just*
> *for the unjust, so that He might bring us to God . . .*
>
> **(1 PETER 3:18, NASB)**

There has to be two huge parts to our justification. First, we have to be forgiven, and secondly, we must receive the gift. For this to happen it is imperative that we receive something that the Bible calls 'righteousness'. Let's have a look and see exactly what we mean.

You Cannot Be Justified Without Being Forgiven

Most times, only the first part (forgiveness of sins) is offered in a gospel presentation, and that so often confusingly. If God does not forgive you your sins, He must then continue to hold them against you, they are a debt on your account. It is quite impossible therefore to go on and be justified at one and the same time be guilty. You're guilty as charged and cannot possibly be acquitted.

So, are we forgiven or not?

Some think ongoing forgiveness is dependent on an ongoing act of confession.

Consequently, they see forgiveness as a changeable state, a flexible condition.

If this is the case, not only have we moved away from grace and started contributing to our own salvation, but our salvation is shaky, very insecure. This constant state of flux means we could lose it at any moment.

Then again, what about sins we have forgotten about and never confessed? And what about sins of omission as well as commission? Things we should have done but never did.

What about things we do that we don't even consider as sin, but God does? Like this following example.

When I was a child, my mother would often say, 'Be sure your sins will find you out'. She told me that this quote was in the Bible. Is it? It is actually, but only once. Who said it and why? And what was this sin so singled out for such a warning? It was said by Moses to two-and-a-half tribes in Israel. What was their grievous sin that made this 'meekest man in all the earth' (Numbers 12:3) so angry? Was it idolatry? Was it immorality? Was it that constant griping and moaning against God?

It was none of these, it was the sin of *non-involvement*. These tribes had prospered greatly and decided that the land on the east side of the Jordon was far better for their tens of thousands of cattle and livestock. So, they made the executive decision that they would not be going into the promised land with the rest of Israel, leaving the nation seriously short staffed for soldiers, givers and warriors. After a threat of judgment by Moses, they agreed to participate in the campaign, only if they could revert to their green pastures later. Moses consented, but with the warning, if you don't move on and in with them, *be sure your sins will find you out* (Numbers 32:23). Today, non-involvement is seen by many Christians as their God-given right, and not as a sin at all. Is that sin forgiven if not even recognized, never mind unconfessed?

The moment we come to God through Christ, and place our faith in Him, we are forgiven once and for all of past, present, and future sins, it's a done deal. It has to happen for me to be justified before God and by God. Unforgiveness and justification by faith cannot possibly be travelling companions, it's one or the other, but not both.

All our sins were forgiven not because they were forgotten, their formidable cost and huge price were paid for on the cross over 2,000 years ago. He took our sins — ALL of them — onto the cross with Him. I don't think that we have any idea how big this forgiveness actually is and how much God has forgiven us. I don't think that we see or have any idea of the depth of our offense towards God. I was not only a sinner in a dirty suit, it was ragged and ripped, one worn by a beggar on the street. I was that man in highways and byways that Jesus spoke of in a parable, certainly not fit to come into any king's banquet.

A story is told of a young commanding officer living and serving in the days of the great Russian empire under the rule of Tsar

Nicholas II. This young man's father was a very close friend of the tsar, and the young officer consequently got a privileged post commanding a military garrison. Regrettably, the officer had a serious gambling addiction and having run out of his own money began to pilfer the garrison funds, thinking he will make up later.

One day, a telegram arrived saying that the tsar himself was coming to visit. In panic he sat late into the night attempting to balance the books and was left shocked and horrified when he realised how much he actually owed. He had no way or any hope of paying it.

The young officer pulled a revolver out of the drawer, thinking a gunshot to the head being the only way out. He looked at his final balance sheet and wrote on the bottom, 'Who can pay such a sum?' He reflected on the shame he had now brought on his father, and asked himself what would his family think? In so doing, and because of the lateness of the hour he fell fast asleep.

It so happened that late into the night, the tsar himself arrived, and on seeing the light on in the office, went in to investigate. There he saw the officer asleep, the gun on the table and the balance sheet with the note *Who can pay such a sum?* written across it. The tsar quickly grasped the situation, and moved with great compassion for the lad, wrote underneath the officer's question, 'Nicholas II can, paid in full'.

Who could ever pay our sinful debt? We were not sick in our sins; we were dead in our sins. Dead men cannot do a thing to save themselves. But the Bible tells us . . .

But God, being rich in mercy, because of His great
love with which he loved us, even when we were
dead in our wrongdoings, made us alive together
with Christ (by grace you have been saved).

(EPHESIANS 2:4–5, NASB)

And now, having been forgiven, they are forgotten.

"For I will be merciful toward their wrongdoings.
And their sins I will no longer remember."

(HEBREWS 8:12, NASB)

Dressed Fit for a King — Righteousness

As good as total forgiveness is, this alone would not have been enough. It would have left us forgiven sinners, but we are actually more than that. We are children of God. Identified as 'saint' in the New Testament.

For justification to be complete, we need to be gifted righteousness. This is a most remarkable truth. Righteousness is, according to the dictionary, a condition of being totally morally right. This is what all religions promise but always fail to deliver. Building hard on the twin towers of hard work and self-effort, often at great personal sacrifice, people try, try and try again to arrive at a place that God offers as a free gift. The unique and lovely offer of the gospel of grace is just this. Having lauded the praises of the gospel in Romans 1:16, Paul goes on to explain the prize possession, the great offer of this gospel in Romans 1:17:

For therein is the righteousness of God revealed from faith to faith: as it is written, the just shall live by faith.
(ROMANS 1:17, KJV)

Instead of having to work up for this in an endless road of non-arrival, we have been given it FREE. And as we read, we accept it by faith.

I discovered that one of God's names in the Old Testament is *Jehovah Tsidkenu* — the Lord our Righteousness. With reference to my earlier story, we must realise that Jesus is my white suit. There are only two ways to get righteousness. You have to do all you can to get it or accept it as a gift from someone who already has it. And Jesus is the ONLY one who has it, and he offers it to you.

Over 200 times, the New Testament tells us that we are IN Christ. We didn't earn our righteousness, it was given to us as a free gift, and even when we get it, it's never ours — it's His. A divine exchange is on offer. We read:

He made Him who knew no sin to be sin in our behalf, so that we might become the righteousness of God in Him.
(2 CORINTHIANS 5:21, NASB)

It always comes back to this: God has done a work for us that we could never do for ourselves. He lifts us up to His level of normality — righteousness.

Since we can't see it, and must believe that this is the case, it seems to be a permanent struggle just to live in that place so that we can then live out that experience. We so easily see our faults and failures, but we must find focus on the new-creation reality.

Paul had a favourite word, **stand.** It was in our opening text . . .

> *Therefore, having been justified by faith, we have*
> *peace with God through our Lord Jesus Christ,*
> *through whom we also have obtained our introduction*
> *by faith into this grace in which we stand . . .*
> **(ROMANS 5:1-2, NASB)**

He repeats this word often through his epistles. It's the Greek word *histémi,* meaning *to stand firm, continue, abide.* The appointing and gifting of righteousness is God's part, but standing by faith in what God has done is our part. And that's when we want to quit and run. Our own inner voice will so often confirm the truth of the accusation when we fail or when we fall, telling us that we are guilty as charged. And we conclude, how can a guilty man be justified? Everything within us wants to **work our way back**. So, penance and penalty are the pathways religion builds. Surely, we must do *something* to earn this righteousness again.

A person must be justified if he is to have any relationship at all with a holy God.

Since righteousness is a condition that God in one redemptive act brings to us, we must conclude that you can't grow in righteousness, you either are or are not righteous. The newest Christian is as righteous as the oldest believer.

This remarkable quality is first *imputed* to us, that is, God acts in such a way that He Himself *declares* us to be righteous. He assigns or designates such an asset to our account. It's a profound pronouncement, something established in the courts of heaven once and for all. It is so important that God records the names of all those who receive it. We read that their names are written in the Lamb's Book of Life. And the names are written in indelible ink, not a pencil with an eraser at its end. Those names cannot be removed.

This is exactly what happened to Abraham in the Old Testament. We read:

> *Then he believed in the LORD; and He*
> *credited it to him as righteousness.*
> **(GENESIS 15:6, NASB)**

But God also imparts it to us by the miracle of new birth. We have already read:

> *He made Him who knew no sin to be sin in our behalf, so*
> *that we might become the righteousness of God in Him.*
> **(2 CORINTHIANS 5:21, NASB)**

Consequently, while our standing before God in heaven is forever settled, our lived-out experience here on earth goes from faith to faith.

The apostle Paul says in Romans 5:1–2: *Therefore, having been justified by faith, we have peace with God through our Lord Jesus Christ, through whom we also have obtained our introduction by faith into this grace in which we stand . . .* (NASB).

So, we must ask, how can God declare those clearly guilty as righteous? And how can He then forever see them as if they had never sinned at all? Not even once! Does He simply ignore the sin? Does He turn a blind eye to it? Or is it simply a whimsical choice He makes one day just because He felt like it?

Does He have executive powers like a president handing out presidential pardons? God is a just judge, He can't turn a blind eye to any sin or any unrighteousness, and neither can He act impartially, treating one different than another. So, our God acts with astronomical grace. What we couldn't do for ourselves He did for us.

It's all and every time grace; God the sole actor and we the blessed receivers.

Repentance and Confession
May Not Be What You Think

We so often run the word *repentance* right alongside *sins*, yet the Bible doesn't actually ever tell us to repent from our sins. It tells us to repent from our 'dead works'.

*. . . Let us press on to maturity, not laying
again a foundation of repentance from dead
works and of faith toward God.*

(HEBREWS 6:1, NASB)

A dead work is any effort on our part to add to God's grace in redemptive activity. We undertake these actions (endless confession, remorse, penances, duties and penalties) because we have some kind of confidence in their meritorious work. They always promise to make us *feel* better but never actually do. They are all powerless to deliver us from sin or a terribly troubled conscience.

In that repentance means a change of mind and heart that leads to a change of direction, we can rightly conclude that its end result always leads to newness of life and away from sin. We are told to forsake our sins, give them up, let them go. We must reach for the high life and let go of the low life. But we always do so from a vantage point of victory.

Confessing Sins?

We are told to confess our sins in 1 John 1:9, which cannot possibly mean as some think — listing them; it means acknowledging that this is our condition, and that we are sinners in need of salvation. I believe that this is consistent with the context of John's letter as he identifies various groups of people that he addresses in his letter. We will talk more fully about this point in another chapter, but these points below are of importance.

Even if we listed every last thing we could think of in order that we could confess them, then that list would be a very, very, very long way from being complete!

Can you recollect every wrong thought, attitude and word that you have ever had or spoken? And that's before we get into actions and activities.

We love grading sins, we confess the 'big' ones, but Jesus told us a lustful thought crosses the line and an angry heart is murderous. If forgiveness hinges on the confession of each and every sinful thought, word, action, or attitude, I am afraid that we have zero chance of ever getting right with God. If we think we can itemize our sins, we have not adequately appraised the low state to which we had fallen and have a far too high opinion of ourselves and our own self-righteousness.

If we think that the Holy Spirit is here to convict us of sins, we should be aware that He will not grade them, and that He would do a thorough job, so thorough that the weight of the conviction would probably kill us.

In fact, even attempting to confess our sins means we believe we have a manageable amount, a limited number, a workable total. We think there are a few, and we should just mention them. But our sins have created a massive chasm between us and our God. Jesus was pointing this out when He told the story of two men at prayer, one thanked God that he wasn't as bad as other men. In Luke 18:11 onwards, we find the Pharisee busy listing his sins, or lack of them, but the tax collector is beating his chest, calling on God for mercy for his many sins, too many to mention and too long to list. It's the latter, said Jesus, who went to his house justified (Luke 18:14).

Those who teach that we must confess and itemize our sins daily are in grave danger of being seriously mistaken about their own standing. Even when we read that Jesus teaches that the Holy Spirit will convict the world of sin (John 16:8), it is *sin* singular, not *sins* plural. We are pre-Christ convicted of our condition, not our activities. Our activities are simply the result of what we are, the rotten fruit from a fallen tree.

I am grateful to N.T. Wright who, in his book *Jesus and the Victory of God,* points out a profound truth about sinners and forgiveness. We often read that Jesus was a friend of *tax collectors and sinners*. He liked being with them, and the Pharisees hated him for that. Because Jesus offered forgiveness to these sinners, the Pharisees wanted to kill him. But just how did the Jews of the day understand sin and forgiveness? We see forgiveness as a pronouncement of a blessing, an utterance made, so we might respond and say 'thank you'. And we then see sins as a list of known misdemeanours. But it wasn't so in the Jewish mind.

To a Jew, a sinner was a man in exile, one who doesn't belong — he had no rights here.

The word 'sinner' comes from the meaning 'a man of the land'. [5] When the Jews in the Old Testament sinned against God, He sent them into exile. They lost their homeland, they were carried off into Babylon, they were exiles, they were sinners. The promise of forgiveness brought by the prophets meant that the sinner would be restored and returned home, accepted into their own land.

When Jesus forgave sinners, He was welcoming them home, no strings attached. The fact that He did this on His own merit and bypassed the gatekeepers (the Pharisees) made them frantic with hate. They saw Jesus as violating the Law, when in fact He was the only one keeping it. This is the exact point made in the Parable of the Prodigal Son. The wayward son went off to a 'far country', he became an exile, but his redemption meant he came home to his father's house. The extravagant forgiveness is seen in the welcome given by the father — arms open wide, gifts and parties and great rejoicing. Meanwhile, the elder brother wanted nothing to do with 'this son of yours', this kind of forgiveness in his mind was embarrassing, too easy and completely unacceptable. Yet it was this astronomical grace that Jesus offered, and those who knew they deserved it the least loved it the most.

*'The ultimate test of our spirituality is the measure
of our amazement at the grace of God'.*

DR MARTYN LLOYD-JONES

4

This I Know: God is for Me

What I believe about God is the most important thing about me.

A.W. TOZER

Some people's idea of God is just too small.

God has received a tremendous amount of slanderous misrepresentation, but we all know that this isn't anything new. It started in the garden of Eden when Satan said to Eve, *Has God really said?* (Genesis 3:1). In other words, God can't be trusted. The question is: *What do you think about God? How do you see Him? What comes into your mind when you think of Him and on Him?*

Around 4,000 years ago, there lived a very wealthy and upright man called Job. He went through a really hard time. It all started when Satan came and presented himself before God. God asked Satan where he had come from. Satan said that he had been roaming the earth. To which God replied, '*Have you noticed Job?'* God obviously had, for He then praises this man for his outstanding life.

Satan did what comes naturally to him, he started accusing. First, he accused Job of selfish motives, claiming this man was God-fearing and upright only because of the favours and blessings he got back from God in return. Furthermore, Satan then accused God of buying Job's loyalty through these blessing bribes. Satan, in effect, accuses God of running a protection racket like some mob outfit. The outcome of this discussion is that Job finds himself being tried and tested.

In examining why he thought this calamity happened, Job said, *"What I always feared has happened to me. What I dreaded has come true."* (Job 3:25, NLT). As far as Job was concerned it was fear that opened the door to his troubles, but his friends thought otherwise.

The biblical book named after Job tells us that while Job tries to make sense of his circumstances, just as we do so often in life, God got much of the blame from those who were meant to help. We read:

> *It came about after the LORD had spoken these words*
> *to Job, that the LORD said to Eliphaz the Temanite,*
> *"My wrath is kindled against you and against*
> *your two friends, because you have not spoken*
> *of Me what is right as My servant Job has."*
> **(JOB 42:7, NASB 1995)**

These friends, usually referred to as Job's comforters, had told him that all his troubles were God's retribution. There must have been, they reasoned, some sin in Job's life that God was judging. So, in other words, all the calamity Job experienced came from God, and it came because God was angry with Job, trying to teach him a lesson and refine his life. When in fact, the book makes clear the calamity came from Satan himself, operating with God's restrictive permission.

But what we do see in this verse is that God gets angry with the comforters because they had 'not spoken of Me what is right'. They misrepresented God, His heart, motives, character as well as His actions as they counseled their friend in his pain and problems. Just the kind of friends you need, right? Whilst God never offers a 'behind the scenes' explanation to Job of his crises, He does want Job to know that he could and should be trusting Him at all times. He wanted Job to know that He, God, was good.

There is still today a great deal of thinking like Job's comforters, people telling us that God is judging this one or that one. We can so easily think it of ourselves when we hit difficult times. *God is judging me*. We can even then add in *I deserve it*.

Just as Satan was Job's accuser then, he is our accuser now. But as we shall soon see, Satan no longer has the right of access to God and is no longer able to accuse us to Him. This amazing gospel of grace has permanently shut Satan out of God's throne room, and at the same time ushered us right in.

These who think and speak of God judging must have missed what the angel said to the shepherds at the first Christmas,

"Glory to God in the highest, and on earth peace, goodwill toward men!" (Luke 2:14, NKJV). The heavenly message was a huge proclamation that everything was changing because Jesus had come. God was announcing peace and good news, not judgement. Even Jesus told us in John 12:47 that He had not come to judge the world. (Not yet anyway.)

Job is probably the oldest story in the Bible, at least as old as Abraham. There was no law or Bible yet, no tabernacle or priesthood, yet amazingly, Job prays the most prophetic of prayers:

"How then can a man be just with God?"
(JOB 25:4, NASB 1995)

If only there were someone to mediate between us,
someone to bring us together.
(JOB 9:33, NIV)

Even then, Job was crying out for a mediator and advocate, an intercessor. He was calling out for the gospel of grace.

Job is a most wonderful book and amazing story. But I want you to see a pattern here. The bottom line is that Satan has a track record in slandering God in the minds and hearts of people. The insurance companies even do it, as they declare natural disasters 'acts of God'. Satan hasn't given up being the 'accuser of the brethren' (Revelation 12:10).

Here is the most amazing truth to consider: What you think about God is the most important thing about you!

The Gospel of God

Paul, a bond-servant of Christ Jesus, called as an apostle,
*set apart for the **gospel of God**, which He promised*
beforehand through His prophets in the holy Scriptures.

(ROMANS 1:1–2, NASB)

The first epistle that we come across in our New Testament is Paul's all-important book of Romans. It's right there after Acts. I think it's listed first amongst the epistles not because it was written first, which it wasn't, but because it lays the foundation for everything that we must understand pertaining to our redemption. And in this first of the epistles, notice the first thing Paul says, He has been 'set apart for the gospel of God'.

In other texts, we see the gospel labelled and identified in various other ways. The gospel of peace, the gospel of the Kingdom, etc. But here, it's very specific — *the gospel of God*. Then, as we read on in the next few verses, Paul makes mention of both Jesus Christ the Son of God and the Holy Spirit.

We read in verse 3, *concerning His Son, who was born of a descendant of David* and then we read in verse 4, *who was declared the Son of God with power by the resurrection from the dead, according to the Spirit of holiness,* (The Holy Spirit) *Jesus Christ our Lord* (Romans 1:3–4, NASB 1995).

In other words, Paul wants us to know that the most amazing rescue mission ever conceived, the one that he is about to expound on in the whole of this epistle, had God behind it. God the Father, God the Son, and God the Holy Spirit — ALL working together for you and me! This is a love worth finding. They are not working against each other but with each other. Neither is one working for us and another against us, as some people seem to believe. The Godhead is fully involved with our salvation and redemption, since all of it is heading for a huge and glorious future. It adds another new and altogether brilliant emphases to Romans 8:31 (NIV), *If God is for us, who can be against us?* This is grace times three.

No other religion in the world has a concept like the Trinity. One God, existing in three persons, all of whom love you and me with a passion. Each, with combined strength and effort, working out an eternal operational plan with no chance of failure, only total success. You and I both are included in this plan. Sheer love, total commitment, relentless grace, extravagant mercy. J.I. Packer said, '*The Trinity is the basis of the gospel, and the gospel is a declaration of the Trinity in action*'. [6]

This is hugely important in that so many people have been sold a lie. Some have been told that God the Father is irate and so angry with them for their sinful lives. His pristine laws and holy ways have been violated to the point of great offense. They understand the gospel to be Jesus coming to pay for their sins and in so doing, 'appease' the Father. But, they think, we will forever need Jesus as a go-between to calm this angry Father down. Consequently, they have little or no connection with Father God. When praying, they only pray to Jesus, or Mary and the saints if they're Roman catholic.

We are living in a fatherless world; fathers have disappeared in so many families. So, the world has a predetermined mindset of an absentee father. Maybe your story was like mine, where my own father took off when I was a toddler. *What is a father?* is a question many people are asking. Not being able to understand an earthly father adds difficulty enough to any reflection on Father God.

Yet these views of God the Father couldn't be further from the truth. It *is* true that we have violated God's laws; it *is* true that we have gone our own way, rejected his divine right over our lives; it *is* true that we deserve judgement and deserve retribution. But this amazing gospel of astronomical grace turns it all on its head — God withholds what we do deserve and pours out all the good that we don't deserve.

The gospel was the Father's idea; He is the one who sent the Son. The most famous verse in the Bible is John 3:16, *"For God so loved the world, that He gave his only Son, so that everyone who believes in Him will not perish, but have eternal life"* (NASB). And do you remember who said those words? It was Jesus Himself.

We must realise that in this vast rescue mission, God the Father was also paying a huge price. He emptied heaven of the best He had, *My beloved Son* God calls Him.

There is no doubt from the gospel records that John was the closest disciple to Jesus, he even refers to himself multiple times as 'the disciple whom Jesus loved', and it was John to whom Jesus entrusted His mother from the cross. Yet this is what this same John wrote:

See how great a love the Father has bestowed on us, that
we would be called children of God; and such we are . . .

(1 JOHN 3:1, NASB 1995)

The Father wants a family, and He did everything possible to include you in it.

Perhaps the most famous of Jesus' parables is called the Parable of the Prodigal Son, but it should be called the Parable of the Amazing Father! We read and then watch this father in the story embrace and kiss his long-lost wayward son.

In the parable, the son, who had left home and squandered his inheritance, hits rock bottom and longs to come home. He has rehearsed his apology and his I'm-no-longer-worthy speech, but this father would hear none of it, didn't even let him get those words out of his mouth. The son is home and that's all that matters. It's party time. *Get him some new shoes, clothes and a ring on his finger.*

This wayward son didn't have to work his way back. It's natural to think the Father should have started out by letting him sleep in the barn, prove his worth, demonstrate that he has *really* repented. But that's not who the father is and it's not what the father does. The boy isn't seen as a servant; he's welcomed as a son. And because he's a son, he gets all the privileges of a son. Remember, Jesus who has perfect knowledge of the Father is the One who told this story, so it is an exact representation of the Father's heart.

Jesus defined eternal life when He said, *"This is eternal life, that they may know You,* (Father), *the only true God, and Jesus Christ whom You have sent"* (John 17:3, NASB, emphasis added).

How well do we know the Father?

Do we see His heart for us in Scripture? Do we recognize His grace? Do we receive His forgiveness? When we pray, do we recite a formula, or do we go to our Father as Jesus taught us to in the Lord's Prayer? When we really know our heavenly Father, we know that nothing could ever keep Him from us.

I heard of a true story from the 1980's Armenian earthquake. It was a huge earthquake that happened just as children arrived at school one early morning. This story was about a 12-year-old boy called Armand.

Each morning before Armand set off for school, his father would tell him that he loved him, and that he would always be there for him. The morning of the earthquake was no different. Before Armand left the house that tragic day, his father once again told him, 'I love you and I'll always be here for you'.

As the earthquake shook the city, the dad heard the terrible sound of crashing buildings, and the aftershocks continued the havoc. The father rushed to the school along with so many parents. When he arrived, there was nothing left standing. Frantically he began to dig with his bare hands, with no diggers or bulldozers on site. He continued for several hours, with his hands bleeding with the effort. People shouted at him to quit, it was pointless, no one could have survived such a tragedy. But the father continued, for 8 hours, then 16 hours, then 24 hours; then at 36 hours he heard voices coming from underneath the rubble.

To their amazement, they found Armand alive with around 20 other children, trapped in a pocket as the buildings collapsed. When Armand saw his father, he turned to the other kids and said, 'See, I told you my father would come'.

For centuries, the prophets foretold that God would come, and at the first Christmas He did. We read:

> *Namely, that God was in Christ reconciling the world*
> *to Himself, not counting their trespasses against them,*
> *and He has committed to us the word of reconciliation.*
>
> **(2 CORINTHIANS 5:19, NASB 1995)**

Everything that happened in the gospel happened because of the Father's great love. Do we have any idea how much He loves us, or the lengths He went to for us?

On the other hand, many people speak of God, but have no concept of His Son. Islam, Judaism and even aspects of the Christian faith all acknowledged God, but either do not know, have not heard or refuse to speak of the Son. But God's Son, Jesus Christ, is the only way to God. No one else came and paid the price for our sins or opened the door for us to heaven. Even if someone offered to do so, they would not have sufficed, for only Jesus lived life as a sinless man, laying down His life so that we might receive life.

It's not about us working towards sinning less, it's all about Him being sinless. He is the answer to Job's prayer, the mediator between God and man. Jesus said, *"For I have come down from heaven, not to do My own will, but the will of Him who sent Me"* (John 6:38, NASB).

Everything in the Old Testament foretells of Jesus' coming, and everything in the New Testament tells of what He did in that coming and the amazing future we now have together. Jesus spoke twice of His task being finished; the mission was accomplished.

I have brought you glory on earth by
finishing the work you gave me to do.
(JOHN 17:4, NIV)

Therefore, when Jesus had received the sour
wine, He said, "It is finished!" And He bowed
His head and gave up His spirit.
(JOHN 19:30, NASB)

Perhaps you have heard already that this word 'finished' is significant, it's the Greek word *teleó* and is defined as: **"to perform, execute, complete, fulfil** (so that the thing done corresponds to what has been said, the order, command, etc.), i.e. with special reference to the subject-matter, to carry out the contents of a command." [7]

Jesus completed to the last everything he was asked to do, and in so doing paid in full for our redemption. There is nothing — not one thing — left to be done. All you and I have to do is receive it.

Then there is the precious Holy Spirit.

We are taught that it was impossible for the Holy Spirt to come and live within us until Jesus completed all that He needed to do, which included His resurrection and ascension.

Jesus is in Heaven with the Father, but the Holy Spirit is with us here on earth. Jesus called Him the Comforter or Counselor, not the accuser and fault finder of our sins as some people seem to think. He would be our power source in life. He is the one who will never leave us nor forsake us.

I was once taught that if I wanted the baptism of the Holy Spirit, then I would need to be holy, since He was the Spirit of holiness. Consequently, I was to search out every sin, and only when sure that I was truly repentant and holy would I be able to receive Him. But the Holy Spirit doesn't live in me because I am holy, but because I am righteous. I have been justified. And this righteousness is not my own, but Christ's.

Another misconception is that holiness means sin and fault free, when in fact it means set apart. Furniture, pots and pans were said to be holy unto the Lord in the Old Testament, they couldn't possibly be sinless, but they were dedicated to God and His purpose. In my early Christian life, holiness was identified as a long list of don'ts. You didn't go to the cinema, you don't smoke, drink or hang out with girls that did. But we all saw people who obeyed all the rules but whose hearts were a million miles from God, and others who were still using some of these things but sold out to God. A Christian convert is not identified primarily by his change of actions, but by his change of affections — actions follow later. God has renewed his heart by the Holy Spirit, who is otherwise known as the Spirit of grace.

(Hebrews 10:29; Zechariah 12:10.) And now, because of that which Jesus did, this Spirit of grace lives in you and me.

As we reflect on the above, it's no wonder Paul wrote that most precious of blessings:

> *May the grace of the Lord Jesus Christ, and the love of God, and the fellowship of the Holy Spirit be with you all.*
> **(2 CORINTHIANS 13:14, NIV)**

There is a divine order in the Godhead. It starts with the Father. It's outworked through the Son who came to glorify the Father. It's activated and empowered by the Holy Spirit, who's tasked with telling, talking and revealing Jesus and all that He accomplished in that great 'it is finished' statement. It is finished because God started it and God completed it, we had nothing at all to do with it. That's why it's grace. We contribute nothing to our salvation. It's all God.

Perfect unity, perfect submission, perfect activity. The Father is glorified by the Son's total obedience, and the Spirit works to reveal at all times what the Son has accomplished and brings in the power to live out what we've learned.

God the Father

The first title (not name) given to God in the Bible is "the judge of all the earth." This was said by Abraham back to God in prayer as they discussed Sodom and Gomorrah. Since there is no higher court in the Universe, what this judge says and does stands and counts.

Here is the thing: it is this judge that *justifies* us. We read:

> *Who will bring a charge against God's*
> *elect? God is the one justifies.*
>
> **(ROMANS 8:33, NASB 1995)**

If God justifies us, there is no one else who can 'unjustify' us. The devil tries, our moral conscience joins in, and sometimes our friends and enemies contribute their penny's worth, but we are forever declared by God to be righteous. It's a permanent state within which we now stand according to Paul. And God did it all — we do not, did not, cannot contribute a thing! We simply receive it by faith and say THANK YOU! The judge was able to justify us not by ignoring our sin, but by judging our sin in Christ on that tree. This new condition gives us huge advantages. Here's the biggest: God sees us as He sees Himself. God treats us as He would treat His Son Jesus.

> *Both the one who makes people holy and those who*
> *are made holy are of the same family. So Jesus is*
> *not ashamed to call them brothers and sisters.*
>
> **(HEBREWS 2:11, NIV)**

It's now possible for this God to live in you, be with you, and work through you. And the biggest gain is heaven! Not when you die, but here and now. God wants you to walk in and out of heaven as if it's your native home. And by this, I mean prayer:

Let us therefore come boldly to the throne of grace, that we may obtain mercy and find grace to help in time of need.
(HEBREWS 4:16, NKJV)

It was Martin Luther who said, 'If you can't come boldly don't bother coming at all'. [8] If God justifies us, this and this alone is our entry right into the throne room of God, not how well we have done or are doing.

We have worked extensively in India for very many years, looking after orphans, widows and planting and building local churches. One time I was in with a few hundred of our pastors in a prayer meeting. They were going for it in their own language — praying, shouting, crying, calling. I thought to myself, *What wonderful passion; what a powerful prayer meeting.*

Then God said to me, 'You're mistaken; ask for some translation'. So, I found one of our English speakers and asked him to translate the prayers and the cries. I discovered that they weren't celebrating, they were pleading like beggars. They were crying, asking God to have pity on their sorry plight. They were asking Him if He actually saw their tears? Did He not care?

They had been converted to Christ but hadn't yet seen or grasped where they stood as far as the Father was concerned. They were praying just like they did to their two million Hindu gods. There is no way that God will respond to prayers like that. I spent the next six months teaching them on what God had actually done, and who and what they had now actually become. Today, most prayer meetings are filled with joy, laughter and great confidence.

We often remember or are asked to remember that God is faithful. He is a faithful God, there is no doubt. But when the Bible speaks of His faithfulness, it puts in number one place His faithfulness to be true to His act and judgement of justifying us! Isn't that astronomical grace?

> *"For I will forgive their wickedness and*
> *will remember their sins no more."*
> **(HEBREWS 8:12, NIV)**

Even if we are being overwhelmed by our sense of failure, the truth is the truth — we are forever justified before God.

God the Son — The Prophet, Priest and King

Some say we can see all that Jesus did and does for us in and though His threefold ministry of prophet, priest and king.

Moses called Him a prophet. We read:

> *The LORD your God will raise up for you a*
> *prophet like me from among you, from your*
> *fellow Israelites. You must listen to him.*
> **(DEUTERONOMY 18:15, NIV)**

Prophets were God's spokesmen. They brought the word of God, from God, to reveal God.

Great emphasis is placed in the Bible on listening to the words of Christ specifically. Even when God's audible voice was heard from heaven, it concluded with *'listen to Him!'* (Mark 9:7).

Hebrews tells us that God has now finally spoken to us in these last days through His Son (Hebrews 1:2). Romans reminds us that faith comes by hearing the words of **Christ** (Romans 10:17). And of course, John calls Him the WORD (John 1:1). Jesus revealed the Father, His love and His way. There is no other way to come to God than through Him. The more we focus on Jesus, the more we see and understand grace.

Jesus is called our great High Priest:

> *Therefore, since we have a great high priest who has ascended into heaven, Jesus the Son of God, let us hold firmly to the faith we profess. For we do not have a high priest who is unable to empathize with our weaknesses, but we have one who has been tempted in every way, just as we are — yet he did not sin. Let us then approach God's throne of grace with confidence, so that we may receive mercy and find grace to help us in our time of need.*
>
> **(HEBREWS 4:14–16, NIV)**

Few of us today really understand what a high priest's role was or now is. In the Old Testament, the high priest would enter the Holy Place just once a year and having made a sacrifice would sprinkle the mercy seat on the ark with blood. This great day of atonement was hugely important.

Firstly, the sacrificial blood of the bulls would cover their sins for another year, and secondly, would ensure God's favor and blessing on the people for the next year. The high priest mediated between God and man — NOT because God was angry, but because God was love. Sinners cannot walk into the presence of God and live. Light always dispels darkness, so a way was needed to be found to allow the one to live with the other. The high priest was the bridge builder.

Then in the Old Testament, this priest could never sit down, only stand, in that he or his replacement needed to come again and again, never finished. But we are told that after Jesus' ascension into heaven, He offered His blood to His Father and sat down at the right hand of God. It's finished, complete, no repeat needed.

> *But our High Priest offered himself to God as a single sacrifice for sins, good for all time. Then he sat down in the place of honor at God's right hand.*
> (HEBREWS 10:12, NLT)

The sitting down is as significant as the temple veil being ripped from top to bottom when Jesus hung on the cross, or as significant as Jesus saying *'It is finished'*. His work is complete.

When John writes, telling us that we have an advocate with the Father (1 John 2:1), he is telling us the same thing. That there is one there in heaven, who just by Him being there represents us.

The image that some people see is that heaven is a court room, and Satan comes to accuse us before God of our recent sins committed. They think 1 John 2:1 portrays Satan as the prosecuting counsel and Jesus as our defending counsel. When and only if we confess our sins can our defence lawyer get to work and argue our case before the judge of all the earth. But this imagery is the furthest thing from the truth. Here's why: Satan has lost all grounds of access to God. He can no longer do what he did with Job.

> *"From this moment on, everything in this world is about to change, for the ruler of this dark world will be overthrown."*
> **(JOHN 12:31, TPT)**

> *And having disarmed the powers and authorities, he made a public spectacle of them, triumphing over them by the cross.*
> **(COLOSSIANS 2:15, NIV)**

Not only has he lost access to God, we can stop him accessing us and our lives.

> *Submit yourselves, then, to God. Resist the devil, and he will flee from you.*
> **(JAMES 4:7, NIV)**

Satan Has Lost His Main Weapon of Accusation

When Jesus defeated and destroyed the devil's work, He ripped away his main activity and key weapon — accusation. Every claim the devil would try to make is cancelled, paid for in full by the blood of Jesus. To even think for a moment that any unconfessed sins are still pending is to completely decry the finished work of Jesus. If that were the case, Jesus couldn't sit down, He shouldn't have said *It is finished*, and the veil should still be there keeping us out of the presence of God. But it is finished, and all of our sins (past, present and future) have already been dealt with. You are either forgiven completely or not forgiven at all.

Jesus isn't only our High priest, He was also our sacrificial lamb, and His blood has done, and is doing, a permanent work. This priestly, mediating ministry is also called intercession.

*Who is the one who condemns us? Christ Jesus is the
One who died [to pay our penalty], and more than that,
who was raised [from the dead], and who is at the right
hand of God interceding [with the Father] for us.*
(ROMANS 8:34, AMP)

*Consequently, he is able to save to the uttermost
those who draw near to God through him, since
he always lives to make intercession for them.*
(HEBREWS 7:25, ESV)

We have come to think of intercession as praying prayers, but it's speaking of something else. It's a position that Jesus has taken, and His position of intercession now guarantees certain things for us.

The late evangelical theologian John Stott also believed that we shouldn't in the first instance think Jesus is literally 'praying' for us, but that His very presence in heaven is in and of itself an act of intercession. It's like a permanent door being held open, or a bridge firmly in place.

The Greek word for intercession is *entugchano*, which comes from *tugchano*, meaning 'to attain or secure an object or end, to make ready or bring to pass. To happen or to affect'. [9] In a similar way that the Old Testament high priest acted as mediator, making sure the people's sins were covered and God's blessing and presence were secured, Jesus does the same but better. He not only covers our sins, He permanently obliterates them, washes them away, and then ever lives to make sure that the grace of the New Covenant is secured and all its many blessings brought to pass in our lives. We read He saves to the uttermost (Hebrews 7:25), meaning He will keep us saved to the very end, make sure we make it to heaven, but also 'to the uttermost' means that all God had planned for us comes to us.

Jesus as King

The biggest issue in becoming a Christian is not accepting Jesus as Saviour, but accepting Jesus as Lord (Romans 10:9). He is Lord regardless, but He then becomes your Lord. We read:

> *For if by the transgression of the one, death reigned through the one, much more those who receive the abundance of grace and of the gift of righteousness will reign in life through the One, Jesus Christ.*
>
> **(ROMANS 5:17, NASB 1995)**

Reigning is the language of a king. In this verse it is said that we are to reign in life, but that is only possible **through Jesus Christ**. He is the source of this abundance of grace. He has conquered all our enemies, including the biggest one of all, death. Not for Himself, but for us. He is the King of all kings, and He is the Lord of all lords.

Jesus is our Lord and King. By submitting ourselves to Him, we are relocated into His kingdom. We are citizens of another place. That's why Jesus told us to seek first the kingdom of God; it becomes our primary focus, our first affection. Then, the life of that kingdom is intended to manifest in our lives here and now.

The Holy Spirit

The precious Holy Spirit, also called the Spirit of Grace, is active in our lives in four principal ways.

First, **before** we become Christians, He convicts us of sin.

And He, when He comes, will convict the world concerning sin, and righteousness, and judgment.

(JOHN 16:8, NASB)

When the Bible speaks of the world, it means all who are not yet in the kingdom. That was us before we came to Christ. The Holy Spirit convicts unsaved people of their sins and their plight. It's only then that they are glad to hear the gospel and respond to it. Otherwise, they see no need of a saviour or salvation, it makes no sense to them. Even this is God's grace towards us.

There isn't one single verse anywhere in the Bible which suggests that the Holy Spirit convicts the Christian of sin. In fact, the Bible teaches the converse, for the second activity of the Holy Spirit is to convince us of righteousness.

When Jesus explained the above verse from John to His disciples, He went on to say:

Concerning sin, because they do not believe in Me; and concerning righteousness, because I go to the Father and you no longer see Me.

(JOHN 16:9–10, NASB 1995)

Since the Holy Spirit is here to help us, comfort us, and to reveal the works of Jesus within us, He is our best friend when we fall and fail. He does not point out the sin but points out the Saviour. We're all too aware of our failing and the discouragement it brings, but the Holy Spirit assures us of our position and settled status before God. We read:

> *If our hearts condemn us, we know that God is*
> *greater than our hearts, and he knows everything.*
> (1 JOHN 3:20, NIV)

Do you remember the gospel account on that sabbath occasion when the Pharisees had a go at the disciples for eating the corn as they walked through the field? According to them, the disciples were 'working' and so violating the fourth commandment. What did Jesus do? When we read the story, we notice that Jesus Himself was not actually eating the corn but went on to defend the disciples before their accusers. Jesus is now in heaven, but the Holy Spirit is right here right now defending us. He wants us to know that even if we're falling short, we can still stand strong, for our status before God does not change.

The Father is not going to send the Son to fully save us, to then have the Holy Spirit working against that amazing work by undermining our confidence in Christ and making us revert to an insecure status, always checking, wondering if enough was done for us. Yet sadly, so much of Christianity is working as if that is the case.

You are either forgiven completely or not forgiven at all.

Thirdly, the Holy Spirit brings transformational power into our lives. We run a biblical leadership college called Destiny College; its moto is *Transformation leads information*. We are being changed, the Bible says, but we are unable to change ourselves. As God comes to live within us, so He then gets to live through us. Galatians 5 tells us of the beautiful fruit of the Holy Spirit that starts growing on the tree of our lives. He is ever-present, helping us to pray when we just don't know how, and He is forever working to conform us to the image of God's Son. That's why it's pointless preaching a Christian lifestyle to non-Christian people. Even if they ever wanted to live it, they just don't have the power to do so. We are called to preach Christ and He brings with Him all transformational power necessary.

Fourthly, the Holy Spirit brings missional power for ministry — supernatural gifts and boldness of spirit. You might know that the Greek word for gifts as listed in 1 Corinthians 12 is *charisma,* where 'charismatic' comes from, but meaning free gifts of grace. You can get to move in a supernatural dimension by sheer grace, nothing earned or worked for. The more we live in grace the more we will move in power.

Deep Water

We once had a super-tanker captain as a member of our church. He always had fascinating stories to tell of his exploits and adventures. One day, he told me about a very difficult and narrow passage they were navigating with such a huge ship. They had taken on board a pilot and were being assisted by several tugs. He was amazed at the pilot's skill in such difficult terrain, and so he asked the man, 'You must know where every rock and every wreck is?' To which the pilot replied, 'Yes, to some degree, but I definitely know where the deep water is'.

Likewise, even when we are going through challenging times, stay in deep water. Some only know how to get into 'hot water', but take the pilot of the Holy Spirit on board and let Him be the navigator. Stay in fellowship with God — Father, Son and Holy Spirit. Live believing 'this I know, God is for me' (Psalm 56:9).

'No believer should be content with hoping and trusting,
he should ask the Lord to lead him into full assurance, so
that matters of hope may become matters of certainty'. [10]

C.H. SPURGEON

5

The Law is Good — Or is It?

'The law tells me how crooked I am.
Grace comes along and straightens me out'.

D.L. MOODY

There is a wave of grace revelation sweeping the earth, but it's creating some friction in the church. But then again it always did.

Those who have begun to see and experience this gospel of grace feel like they have been born again . . . again. They feel a huge wave of relief and gratitude; it's a game changer in their Christian walk. Consequently, these people are often left not wanting anything further to do with the law, at all, ever. They would wholeheartedly agree with Thomas Manton who said, *'They have no grace that can be content with a little grace.'* [11]

But sometimes the same people can become pretty grace-less towards those who are still standing where they once stood. Whilst the old guard denounce these 'grace extremists' as re-runners of an old heresy (Antinomianism), they, the grace appreciators, can quickly denounce those without a revelation of grace as judgemental, legalistic slave traders who trade in the soul suffering of too many Christians.

But maybe a proper understanding of the law will help us all?

There are two potential pitfalls when it comes to the law — there always has been. Those who make too little of the law — and those who make too much of it.

We need to understand that law and grace are not opposites, it's not either/or, but they are intended as co-workers in one amazing gospel. It's a team effort that could only have been conceived by an all-loving, immutable God.

Walter J. Chantry saw this when he wrote and said *'The law and the gospel are allies, not enemies'.* [12] Both come from the same God, found in the same Bible, and they were intended to work in tandem. In fact, we shall see that there is so much grace in the giving of the Law. We read:

> *So then, the Law is holy, and the commandment*
> *is holy and righteous and good.*
> **(ROMANS 7:12, NASB)**

One group will read this Scripture text and quickly point out its clear statements saying, *So, if the law is 'good' then it should be both kept and applied, and applied rigorously.* But this view would show that there is little or no understanding on *how* the law is good. Perhaps it can be summed up in this quote by Thomas Adams who said, '*The law gives menaces; the gospel gives promises*'. [13]

The law is good, BUT here's the thing: it's not good for everything.

The Law came from God, through angels, (Acts 7:53, Galatians 3:19) was delivered unto Moses, who in turn delivered it (twice) to the children of Israel. Not only did God give them the moral law (The Ten Commandments), but He gave them a ceremonial law, filling up the books of Leviticus and Numbers and found in several other places in the Bible. We don't usually like reading these books, or only read them if we must when they're in our reading plan for the year.

It's in these books that we find morning and evening sacrifices, ashes of red heifers, multiple offerings, feasts and special days, heaps of instructions about washings, fabrics that should or shouldn't be worn or food that can or cannot be eaten. What do these have to do with us we ask? Some dismiss the records as simply God's health and safety hygiene laws for a bygone era. I know some Christians who don't even read the Old Testament, thinking that somehow only the last and latest part of the Bible is important today.

Such people make too little of the Law.

For as the old saying goes, *The New is in the Old concealed and the Old is in the New revealed.* All of the Bible — including these parts — are Holy Spirit inspired, and all of the Bible speaks of Christ. There are so many treasures to be found in those same pages.

There is one God, and He has *always* been a God of grace. If the Law came from Him, then it must be good and relevant for us today. And in fact, Jesus endorsed this view in Matthew 5 when he said:

> *"For truly I say to you, until heaven and earth*
> *pass away, not the smallest letter or stroke shall*
> *pass from the Law until all is accomplished."*
> (MATHEW 5:18, NASB 1995)

Making Too Much of the Law

God Himself gave the Law. Moses didn't make it up, the people didn't imagine it, and as we read, it *is* good (Romans 7:12). But here's the thing, it's not good for everything.

Some expect too much of the law, thinking that it can indeed save them, others believe the law is the all-important raison d'etre of life. Yet others think since we were unable to keep the law as fallen sinners, we must get saved and that's only by grace; but thereafter, once saved by grace, then law takes over and once again lays its demands, only now even more rigorously in that as a Christian, I should know better.

But God never gave the law to save anyone. It's not our reason for living, and in fact as we shall see, we are permanently freed from the law — all of it. God didn't give the law to make you acceptable in His sight. In fact, the converse is true, the law condemned us.

In the days that God gave the law through Moses, He was already living amongst His people. He supernaturally saved them from Pharaoh, He supernaturally sustained them and covered and protected them on the way. That was grace right there — tangible, visible and touchable.

Grace gives what we don't deserve, and these people were definitely undeserving of anything whatsoever from God, yet this kindness and goodness flowed unabated, putting food in their stomachs, keeping clothes on their backs and even shoes on their feet. However, they were failing miserably as far as the law was concerned. No one can be saved by the law or brought one inch closer to God by keeping it. In fact, things went terribly wrong with Israel after the giving of the law. We read that 3,000 died in one day!

I have heard it said, and read in some books, that when the New Testament so clearly teaches we are now no longer under law but under grace, it only means the ceremonial law. The thought is that we are freed from the ceremonial law, but the moral law still stands, making its full and just demands and shouting out its obligations that must still be met.

But such an argument could never stand once you have read the book of Romans or Galatians and heard and felt Paul's passionate pleas and such clear teaching. I am hoping that by the time you finish this book you will see that you are free from it all.

You cannot rely on the law for salvation or for intimacy with God, and certainly not to gain favor with Him. But still so many churches today are preaching Moses instead of Jesus.

John 1:17 says, *"For the Law was given through Moses, grace and truth were realized through Jesus Christ"* (NASB). This verse marks a change of era, it's a game changer.

The law is like a mountain that challenges you to climb it. It speaks of hard work and self-effort, particularly to attain righteousness. Many people have, and still are attempting that climb. But when we look at the very first mention of a mountain in the Bible, we discover that man didn't have to climb it, he was actually brought to rest on top of it. That was Mt Ararat, of course, with Noah and his family. Right there we are given a picture of the gospel of grace: Jesus is our ark, and we are repositioned safely in life.

There are two words that should demand our attention, they are *attain and obtain*. What we couldn't attain, we can obtain anyway, all and only through Jesus.

The law is a human effort endeavor. Few people realise that this "human effort" method of salvation had already been tried by God with Adam. God made a covenant with Adam, which is usually called a *covenant of works*. God would promise certain blessings to Adam, if Adam in return did certain things and kept some basic commands. But Adam, even in his perfect, pre-fall state, couldn't keep his side of the contract. Adam and Eve utterly failed and utterly fell. And such has been the story ever since.

If Adam, in a perfect state, couldn't keep one command, what about all of us who came after him, born into sin and with sin? What chance do we have of keeping the Ten Commandments? God already knew what would happen with Adam and Eve. God knew that it would turn out that way for we read:

And all that dwell upon the earth shall worship him,
whose names are not written in the book of life of the
Lamb slain from the foundation of the world.

(REVELATION 13:8, KJV)

Jesus was not 'plan B', grace is not the last resort, but the first factor in an eternal sequence of salvation events that has caught us up in it. God is not taking us back to pre-fall Adamic days, He is taking us forward to a glorious new age.

God knew no man was ever going to be able to keep the law, even before it was given. Especially as man was now spiritually dead with no life and no power within him to do so. In Ephesians 2:5, God didn't say we were sick in our sins, He said we were dead in our sins, dead-dead-dead! A lost cause, this is a worse-case scenario. Can a dead man do anything — except stink? And when we decide that we are going to live by the law, we usually end up stinking too! We smell badly of self-righteousness, hypocrisy and judgemental attitudes.

Sadly, all too often, that is the smell the sinners have smelt when they have come near our churches.

Paul writes the same when he said, *"For what the Law could not do . . . God did: sending His own Son . . ."* (Romans 8:3, NASB). So, God was not about to rerun such a plan as the one with Adam, a plan that depended on human effort, or in fact a plan that depended on any human input at all. He had already made this clear with Abraham. This plan of redemption was unfolding and with God as the sole actor, this was not then or ever intended to be a journey of man's best effort.

God was unfolding a way of working with man, where He would do absolutely everything. All that man was going to have to do was receive this great offer by faith, and even the faith came from God in the first place.

For by grace you have been saved through faith;
and that not of yourselves, it is the gift of God; not
as a result of works, so that no one may boast.
For we are His workmanship, created in Christ
Jesus for good works, which God prepared
beforehand so that we would walk in them.
(EPHESIANS 2:8-10, NASB 1995)

Notice we are saved FOR good works, not BY good works. Paul understood this better than anyone, for he had spent his life trying to attain God's approval by keeping the law. Until, that is, grace met him on that Damascus Road and knocked him off his donkey. Grace opened his eyes whilst temporarily removing his sight. Paul, like Martin Luther after him, searched for this elusive place of 'justification', never once finding it in the law, but overwhelmed when receiving it by grace.

In one form or another, salvation by works finds its way into all religions except genuine Christianity. It's what makes it different, unique and breathtakingly lovely. The gospel is good news, God reaching down to us when we could never reach up to Him. Yet, even today, millions of Christians are trapped in a dark misunderstanding, working hard every day, trying their best to appease and please God by looking to the law in an unending quest to perform it or keep it, or their version of it. *If God requires it then I must do it*, they think and say just as the children of Israel so quickly said in Exodus:

> *Then all the people answered together and said,*
> *"All that the LORD has spoken we will do."*
> (EXODUS 19:8, NKJV)

But of course, they didn't do it, because they couldn't do it. They were utterly powerless to do so, and God already knew this. They, like us, did not realise this at the time, nor did they fully appreciate their utter hopeless and helpless state. They thought they *could* keep the law, that's why they said what they did. They were just like millions of people today who think that they can keep it and are determined to give it their best try, not realising the harder they try to keep the law, the *further* they go from God.

No wonder millions of Christians are depressed. No one is further from God than those who see themselves as morally upright, believes it's their duty to be so, and continually tries to produce that life by hard work and self-effort.

This was the problem with the Jews in Jesus' day. They took pride in the law. They were not, they thought, like the Gentile dogs, lawless heathens. They made a very big deal of keeping the law, it was the very thing that made them different from the rest of the world. They had a covenant with God and the rest of the planet did not. It is no wonder that the Pharisees violently reacted and clashed with Jesus, because He was taking from them the very thing within which they trusted. They were so married to the law that they in all sincerity could not believe that God was behind Jesus' teaching, actions and powerful life. To them it was inconceivable that this could be God at work. They were sincere about this, but sincerely wrong.

In the wilderness, the children of Israel needed to see the depths of their plight. And so, the law begins to work out its role, teaching and training and pointing forwards to a permanent fix for the desperately dark and totally lost human condition. That's why God gave the law even when knowing they (or us) had no possibility of keeping it. The giving of the law was in itself an act of great grace.

Therefore the Law has become our tutor to lead us
to Christ, so that we may be justified by faith.
(GALATIANS 3:24, NASB 1995)

It's the reason why God, at one and the same time, gave them the ceremonial law alongside the moral law. Knowing they could never keep the moral law, He instigated a system and process to deal with their certain and impending failures. That was an act of grace right there again, God making a temporary way until the time was right for the eternally intended plan of redemption to play out its astronomically wonderful drama outside the city wall of Jerusalem.

The washings and the sacrifices and the endless shedding of blood of tens of thousands of bulls, lambs and goats — all of it to teach them, and us, some very important things. We should note that we did not read earlier that the law *was* good but *is* good. So whatever good was in it then, is in it now.

In that law and grace work together, and we have already said that the law is good but not good for everything, let's take a look at the law's role in grace's mission.

This Is How the Law Is Good and Designed To Work

a: To bring man to a state of conviction
The law revealed God's nature and expectations. That is the standard required if we are to be as He is and so enjoy that intimacy with the God of the Universe. To fulfil the heavenly quest and God's deepest desire, we read *"They shall be My people, and I will be their God"* (Jeremiah 32:38, NASB). In so doing, the brightness of the law's light shines into the furthest recesses of my own heart, showing the utter depravity of my own condition. The law points a finger at me and blasts out 'guilty'.

> *What shall we say then? Is the Law sin? May it never be! On the contrary, I would not have come to know sin except through the Law; for I would not have known about coveting if the Law had not said, "YOU SHALL NOT COVET."*
> **(ROMANS 7:7, NASB 1995)**

Once as a child, I was given a large, powerful flashlight as a Christmas present. It came ready to go with brand new batteries. I could not wait for it to get dark that day, because the strength of the flashlight was almost unnoticeable in daylight. I even hid in a cupboard to try it out. But once darkness came, that flashlight shone like a beacon into the night. Similarly, I could not have seen the dazzling brilliance of God's extravagant love or the magnitude of His grace without first seeing the darkness of my own soul. The law first floodlights me and finds me seriously wanting. The law is for sinners. That they might be aware of their plight.

But grace overwhelms us with its breathtaking generosity of forgiveness and acceptance. Without the law we would never truly appreciate grace.

But the law does not stop at pointing the finger. Because of the undeniable truthfulness of its claim, it also opens the terrible troubling doors of guilt and condemnation. And these in turn become weapons of choice for the adversary of our souls who revels in our plight, for he well knows that a Christian walking and living in condemnation will be a completely ineffective Christian.

This Christian never believes that God can use him for anything or would ever answer his prayers. The biggest lie the devil sells is that you are not fully forgiven, at best only partially so. And even if you were forgiven, today was another fresh day when the law was applied and you failed again; so you're guilty again, only more so because by now you should know better, you should have tried harder. This is the worst hamster wheel on earth. It's the Groundhog Day story of many a Christian.

But once grace enters, we find sheer delight in Romans. In chapter 8 we read:

There is therefore now no condemnation
for those who are in Christ Jesus.
(ROMANS 8:1, ESV)

This verse could read from the Greek as follows:

There is therefore now no, no, no, no, or ever can be
any condemnation for those who are in Christ Jesus.

This small two letter word 'no' is taken from the Greek word *oudeis* which is a powerful negating conjunction. It rules out for always and ever, every possibility; it permanently shuts the door to accusation and condemnation. It means that this is such an absolute fact that no valid exception exists to negate it.

b: The prison of law makes us long for freedom

The Bible itself sees the law as a prison, a detention centre, locking us up until the full revelation of the gospel of grace by faith arrived.

But before faith came, we were kept in
custody under the law, being shut up to the
faith which was later to be revealed.
(GALATIANS 3:23, NASB 1995)

It hemmed us in, left us nowhere to go to find peace and rest for our thirsty souls. But the good news is that we don't need to be in that prison any longer. It's like Jesus said to the crowd around Lazarus after he had raised him from the dead, *"Loose him, and let him go"* (John 11:44, NKJV).

The Bible makes it crystal clear:

> *But now we have been released from the Law, having died to that by which we were bound, so that we serve in newness of the Spirit and not in oldness of the letter.*
>
> **(ROMANS 7:6, NASB)**

All men are searching for peace. They will never find it until they find their peace with God. They are trapped. As I write in a middle of a global pandemic, the most Googled word presently is 'prayer' or 'praying'. People are desperate. But we are in lockdown of life and lockdown of heart. I have never seen so many people standing still in one place, but with endless restlessness of an empty spirit.

There is no escaping a guilty conscience. We can engage with a works-based so called spiritual journey offered by sects, cults and religions the world over; it promises that tomorrow we will arrive. Just one more step. If we can get up that one more level. Just keep trying. Always promising, never delivering.

Today, man is trying his hardest to eradicate the notion of sin altogether, but the law is unmovable. The German philosopher Nietzsche already tried this more than a hundred years ago. He made the big announcement that *God is dead* and argued that the belief in the Christian God had become unbelievable. He predicted and prophesied that the whole of European morality is determined to collapse. Our own morality he argued, was a self-induced psychosis of the mind propagated by religion, and we would soon grow out of it. He ended up mentally sick for most of his life and died relatively young. It is said that his ideas profoundly affected Adolf Hitler, and history records that dreadful result.

We foolishly think that if we remove God, we can remove God's law. But we read:

> For the wrath of God is revealed from heaven against all ungodliness and unrighteousness of men who suppress the truth in unrighteousness, because that which is known about God is evident within them; for God made it evident to them.
>
> (ROMANS 1:18–19, NASB 1995)

I am guilty as charged, and deep down inside I know it. But where can I go to escape, to whom shall I turn? I long to get out of this prison, who has the key? Grace shouts, 'I do!'

c: To show us the exceeding sinfulness of sin

In Romans 8:2, Paul calls it *the law of sin and death*. Sin is not a list of God's pet hates, but a vile and hideous force, which in every occasion leads to death. God wants you to live, so He is against everything that leads to death.

Look back into the Old Testament and see all that blood, all those sacrifices, the perpetual daily grind of killing and burning, the hands laid on innocent lambs, the scapegoats sent out to die in the wilderness. Why? Because there were consequences to violating the law, and those consequences were costly.

Too often, the grace enthusiasts are accused of belittling sin. Critics say it now, and they said it to Paul. In reply, Paul said:

What shall we say then? Are we to continue
in sin that grace may increase?
May it never be! How shall we who died to sin still live in it?

(ROMANS 6:1–2, NASB 1995)

The truth is, I became very aware of my own sinfulness, and tried for years to get away from it. But wherever I went, I was there. The law had done its work in me. I am so intensely passionate about the gospel of grace because of the agony of mind and soul that sin, when lit up by the law, produced in my life.

The law is meant to do a work in people — and this is a part of it — we are utterly depressed about the plight of our own situation. Those who come into grace, do so because the law has done a good heart work in them. The more passionate people are about the law and believe mistakenly in its meritorious worth, haven't as yet, in my view, come to the place where the law has done its work within them. When the law has done its work, and you arrive at that point, you can't wait to get away from it, and have no desire to run towards it.

d: To teach us that we need forgiveness

We find it difficult to comprehend the full burdensome weight of living under a ceremonial system. A never-ending walk of acknowledging our sin, a permanent journey of bringing penance. Morning and evening sacrifices. Sin conscience day and night. Every day I would be reminded of my failure, I would be asking, isn't there a **permanent** fix?

Can you imagine going to the temple or tabernacle to seek forgiveness and taking along your perfect sacrificial lamb? To then go through the slaying-shedding-offering by the priest, only to find that on your way home you have an altercation with a neighbour and then say things that you later regret. Before you get home, you would need to go back for further forgiveness.

Whilst we don't go to the temple anymore, too many are spending their morning and evening saying sorry to God and promising to do better tomorrow. They have been sold a lie that tells them the only sins which can be forgiven are those that get confessed.

Furthermore, they have been told that the Holy Spirit's role within them is finger-pointing so that we can become very aware of the sins we might have missed. They attribute to the Holy Spirit the very thing that the law itself was designed to do. This is a terrible indictment on God and the gospel. Forgiveness from God is full, final and absolute already. He provided forgiveness for us before we were born, but today we receive it by faith.

In fact, the Bible teaches us the exact opposite of what some Christians teach. We read:

Who will bring a charge against God's
elect? God is the one who justifies.
(ROMANS 8:33, NASB 1995)

God the Holy Spirit is not pointing out our sins, He's pointing out our justification. He will never bring a charge against us, since that would in effect say Christ's death was insufficient. In fact, He is telling us, even when we're wrong, we're right before God! We are right with God, because we're standing in unblemished, spotless, Christ-given righteousness, which can never fade, never get stained and never fail.

There isn't one single Bible verse that ever tells us that the Holy Spirit's role in the life of a Christian is conviction of sin — not one. Yet, it is believed as standard doctrine. Of course, Jesus did say that the Holy Spirit would convict the world of sin, always pointing people to a Saviour.

The most remarkable aspect of grace is seen when we may be at our worst. Having perhaps sinned and failed again, God still says stand, the righteousness on you hasn't faded, hasn't failed, hasn't evaporated. It hasn't deteriorated, it hasn't been contaminated or diluted, it hasn't contracted or been decommissioned. This righteousness is still perfect and pure, for it is the very righteousness of God.

e: To teach us that we need power

> *You were dead in your offenses and sins,*
> *in which you previously walked . . .*
> **(EPHESIANS 2:1–2, NASB)**

The law shows us that not only are we too weak to keep it, but hopelessly beyond that, we're dead with no possibility of resuscitation. When the law does its work, we realise that we are powerless against sin. We are like the man trying to get out of quicksand; the more effort he exerts, the deeper he sinks, and the more trapped he becomes. Paul puts it this way:

> *For I do not do the good I want to do, but the evil*
> *I do not want to do — this I keep on doing.*
> **(ROMANS 7:19, NIV)**

Anyone who has ever done a 12-step addiction recovery program will immediately identify with this having come to the very first step: *We admitted we were powerless over alcohol and that our lives had become unmanageable.* Well, you come to God the same way, and admit that you are powerless. But here's Jesus' amazing promise:

> *But you shall receive power when the*
> *Holy Spirit has come upon you . . .*
> **(ACTS 1:8, NKJV)**

This is a hugely important point. The law could never bring me to the place where the Holy Spirit would be able to live inside me. I believe in the baptism of the Holy Spirit; I am baptized in the Holy Spirit. I have prayed for very many people to receive the baptism of Holy Spirit. I very often find that if there is a delay or a postponement or any difficulty in bringing someone through into that experience, it is always this: When they rely on the law or their personal holiness performance to receive it, it will keep evading them.

It evaded me for a while, because I was reminded that since He is the **Holy** Spirit, I needed to be holy to receive Him. People told me to come back for prayer when I had searched my own heart, repented of every perceived sin and done all I could to be holy, for then and only then would I receive the baptism of the Holy Spirit. And guess what? Nothing happened.

Then one day it dawned on me, I don't get the Holy Spirit because I am holy, but because I am righteous. It's that unique quality that makes my body a suitable habitation for the Spirit of God. And where did I get this kind of righteousness? One thing is for sure, I did not get it from the law. I got it from Christ.

He made Him who knew no sin to be sin on our behalf,
so that we might become the righteousness of God in Him.
(2 CORINTHIANS 5:21, NASB 1995)

f: To teach us that the law was not ever enough
Paul once made a very powerful claim:

. . . as for zeal, persecuting the church; as for
righteousness based on the law, faultless.
(PHILIPPIANS 3:6, NIV)

He was actually living out the law faultlessly, while at the same time breathing threats and murder against Christians. He did not see it as violent aggression; he saw it as carrying out the ceremonial law, which taught that he should stone and stop heretics. But even though he was faultless before the law, he recognized it was worth nothing. In fact, he called it all *skubalon*: refuse, dregs, or *dung*, and the literal meaning of this word in the Greek is 'what is thrown to the dogs'. [14]

For much of his life, Paul had been taught and trained in all matters of the ceremonial and moral law. He was an expert in knowing it and disciplined in living it. But once he found Christ, he threw it all to the dogs. In my imagination, I see him pulling out his degrees and diplomas obtained at Gamaliel's university and tossing them into the bin — worthless, the lot of it.

Again, you don't have to read the prophetic books of the Bible very long before you come across the protesting of the prophets, railing against people who kept the law, but were a million miles from God. They brought their daily sacrifices but lived self-seeking, God-excluding lives shown through their daily choices.

You take no delight in sacrifices or offerings.
Now that you have made me listen, I finally understand —
you don't require burnt offerings or sin offerings.
(PSALM 40:6, NLT)

These Old Testament Jews thought that the practising of the law was more important than the condition of their hearts. In fact, they went further and thought that their sacrifices and offerings covered over the deliberate disobedient choices and incessant idol worship.

Are we any different today? For some it's easier to give a buck than give their hearts and souls.

God was never after our performance. He is after our hearts, and these hearts have to be renewed, born again by the Spirit of God and saved by the transforming power of the gospel. The law, even if kept as Paul claimed he did, was never ever going to be enough. God has always been after our hearts and affections.

g: The law defines grace for us

The relentless demands of the law demonstrate to us that we can do nothing, bring nothing and add nothing to God's redemptive plan. It's like the verse within the hymn 'Rock of Ages' . . .

Nothing in my hands I bring,
Simply to Thy cross I cling;
Naked, come to Thee for dress,
Helpless, look to Thee for grace:
Foul, I to the fountain fly,
Wash me, Savior, or I die.

Grace is all God; He is the sole actor in our salvation. We didn't even start the process with a call for help from our own hearts or even have any desire to go looking for Him. Romans 5:8 tells us, *"But God demonstrates His own love toward us, in that while we were yet sinners, Christ died for us"* (NASB 1995).

The human heart finds this so difficult. We always want to add something, bring something. We find it almost too difficult to accept that grace is free. Surely, we think, God's forgiveness cannot be unconditional; at least we must deeply repent or confess constantly. And so we turn these acts into grace preconditions — we reduce God's response to being dependent on our actions or depths of our intentions. We continually bring Old Covenant prayers to a New Covenant table. Every time we bring an Old Covenant prayer, with 'ifs' in it, we are moving from grace and back into the law. Grace removed all the 'ifs.'

h: The law foretells of Jesus

We have already quoted in an above point Psalm 40:6, telling us that God was never interested in the sacrifices and burnt offerings, but the same Psalm goes on to prophesy concerning Jesus Himself.

> Then I said, "Behold, I come;
> In the scroll of the book it is written of me.
> I delight to do Your will, O my God;
> Your Law is within my heart."
>
> (PSALM 40:7–8, NASB 1995)

Moses knew it too. He wrote in Deuteronomy 18:15: "*The LORD your God will raise up for you a prophet like me from among you, from your countrymen; to him you shall listen*" (NASB).

So, it is no accident that John connects the two when he writes:

> For the Law was given through Moses; grace and
> truth were realized through Jesus Christ.
>
> (JOHN 1:17, NASB)

Why do we look back to the law, for even when we get back there, the law and the prophets say look forwards? The one promised has now come:

And the Word became flesh and dwelt among us,
and we beheld His glory, the glory as of the only begotten
from the Father, full of grace and truth.
(JOHN 1:14, NKJV)

i: The law modelled substitution
There is another unique way the law works with grace: it points forwards to Jesus as our substitute.

The law modelled the concept of a substitute. Substitution is a stand in, someone or something that can take your place, and in this case, stand in for you in such a way that it takes (or *He* takes) that sin from you by paying the penalty due. And we are told that the wages of sin is death (Romans 6:23).

Of course, it was always temporary in the Old Testament. The substitute was only useful until the next time. But yet the idea was set and established. The Bible says:

For the life of a creature is in the blood, and I have given
it to you to make atonement for yourselves on the altar;
it is the blood that makes atonement for one's life.
(LEVITICUS 17:11, NIV)

The idea of atonement was graphically portrayed every time a sacrifice took place, every time a lamb or other creature was sacrificed. It was to be much later when a moment arrived that John the Baptist pointed at Jesus and said those world chang- ing words, *"Behold, the Lamb of God who takes away the sin of the world!"* (John 1:29, NASB).

The odd thing is that so often, highly intelligent people fail to comprehend this concept. 'How can one die for the sins of another?' they ask. Yet that is the great claim of grace working in redemption. One did die, Jesus — the Son of God died for His own people. And just like all those earlier lambs, this one had to be without spot or blemish. Morally and spiritually.

j: All are made equal under the law

The Jews thought it unbelievable that they were just as lost and just as guilty as the Gentiles, that the only way that they would find salvation was also through the grace of God. Their law was never going to be enough. But they were not the only ones with that problem.

Today we love to grade our sins, that this sin is worse than that one, and we are morally better than our neighbour. In recent decades, the gay community has been the sin-bashing trans- gression of choice. It's no wonder that they have become bitter enemies of many churches. One pastor friend when asked a few years ago if he allowed gays into his church replied that of course he did, he sat them right beside the fornicators over there.

Then again, we are now living in an age with a number of conflicting ideologies that challenge that we are all sinners, fallen and helpless. We read that *all have sinned and fall short of the glory of God* (Romans 3:23, NIV). Virtue signalling is a modern pandemic. Ranging from environmental issues to taking the knee for the Black Lives Matter movement, the world rages against one another on issues of their self-designed, pick-and-mix morality. Yet it's God's law that does and will stand as the final arbitrator; it's an equal opportunity litigator of sin and God's just demands. And unlike critical theory doctrines that are stalking the earth at the moment, God holds one man responsible for his own sins, not for those of his race, history or colour.

Yet the law makes every last one of us equal, equally lost, equally dead, equally debased, equally responsible. We read:

Because by the works of the Law no flesh will be justified in
His sight; for through the Law comes the knowledge of sin.
(ROMANS 3:20, NASB 1995)

Where Does the Evidence Take Us?

The apostle Paul points out a really interesting truth when he writes to the Galatian church. He asked them:

So then, does He who provides you with the
Spirit and works miracles among you, do it by
works of the Law, or by hearing with faith?
(GALATIANS 3:5, NASB)

The Galatian church, despite their reputation for legalism, were experiencing miracles, the supernatural was at work in this church. Paul asks them a 'reminder' question. *Are these amazing things happening because of your law keeping, or because of your faith?* Obviously, it's the latter. The law cannot produce one miracle, but grace operating through faith is a game changer.

We read in Exodus that 3,000 died in one day at the inauguration of this law, but we read 3,000 were saved in one day at the outpouring of the Holy Spirit on the day of Pentecost. We read that Moses' first miracle was turning water into blood, pronouncing judgment, and we later read that Jesus' first miracle was turning water into a wine celebration.

So, we conclude, the law is good, but not good for everything. It always has and always will point to something far greater — the astronomical grace of God. We must distinguish between the words 'attain' and 'obtain'. We can never *attain* or earn God's gracious help, forgiveness, salvation or righteousness by 'law trying' or 'law keeping' for they will always lead to law-induced desperation. But we can *obtain* with full confidence the assurance of all of these things and more by faith in His finished work of total grace.

'The law discovers the disease.
The gospel gives the remedy'. [15]

MARTIN LUTHER

6

The Power of a Good Conscience

'There is nothing beyond being in Christ'.
DR MARTYN LLOYD-JONES

We all have a conscience. It's that inner voice which offers an opinion on all our decisions and actions — past, present and future — both actual and intended. Over and over, it comments and reviews. It not only offers an opinion such as *I wouldn't do that,* but it also raises questions such as W*hy are you doing that?* Our conscience works at the deepest level, questioning our motives along with our actions

Someone once said, ***Every man has a public life, a private life and a secret life.*** The conscience operates in that secret life zone. The Bible says: *No one can know a person's thoughts except that person's own spirit, and no one can know God's thoughts except God's own Spirit* (1 Corinthians 2:11, NLT).

This voice then, is not God's voice. It's not the Devil's voice. It's not even your primary vocal voice, but this voice is a part of who you are. This is the voice of your conscience. This voice comes from so deep within that the Bible frequently refers to it as your heart. This voice comes from your soul as it informs your mind and challenges your spirit.

It's right here, in this very place, that we have to learn one of the hardest things in life — how to live with ourselves. In the Introduction, I made reference to a book by Thomas Brooks, *Precious Remedies Against Satan's Devices*. Brooks preached that the Christian must always remember, four important things:

1. The work and person of our Lord Jesus Christ
2. The Bible, the source of truth
3. The condition of our heart
4. Satan's attacks and devious devices.

All four are important here.

It is within the heart, conscience or inner life that many believers face their biggest battles. 1 John 3:21 says, *Beloved, if our heart does not condemn us, we have confidence before God* (NASB). But the trouble is that our hearts do condemn us all too often. Which means that very many Christians do not have confidence before God. They have no confidence that God could use them in any meaningful way, that their witness and testimony could be effective and fruitful, or that their prayers would get answered or change much at all. They have no confidence then in the promises of God, since their conscience has already disqualified them from being a worthy recipient of such kindness.

And here's the biggest problem, our conscience is usually telling us the truth when it condemns us; it's not fabricating our shortcomings and failures. But is it telling us the *whole* truth?

The apostle Paul was familiar with this struggle. He wrote, O *wretched man that I am! Who will deliver me from this body of death?* (Romans 7:24, NKJV). Martin Luther, the great reformer, was tormented by his conscience, he often wrote and spoke about his tried, tested and battled conscience. He claimed the devil could use the conscience to make the believer impotent, ineffective and fruitless. But then again significant revivals have often been hallmarked by the serious troubling of people's conscience.

In 1630, a great event took place in Shotts, Scotland. John Livingston preached a sermon on a cold Monday morning. Such was its effect that very many people were deeply troubled in conscience to the point they remained in that state of torment for many days. Some were found lying under hedgerows crying out in agony of soul. Others went and knocked on the minister's door in the early hours of the morning, looking for someone to help them find peace in their minds and hearts.

In 1949, on the island of Lewis in the Outer Hebrides, a revival broke out. It is said that over 200 young men turned up together at the local police station. They were looking for someone or something to help them find relief for their troubled consciences and disturbed souls, and having tried the chapel they found it shut, so they hoped that the police constable might help.

John Bunyan in his book *Grace Abounding to the Chief of Sinners*, tells that he was beside himself with inner turmoil for months as he agonised internally, until that is, he came upon grace, and not just grace, *grace abounding.* [16]

We may not have experienced a troubled conscience to that degree, but it still brings a spiritual headache, or at least a heartache. How then can we live with a conscience that reminds us all too often of how faulty and frail we are? And how do we move forward into this wonderful world of grace and faith? It's not just knowing that you are saved but being able to thoroughly enjoy the fact that you are saved.

Your conscience, to use a modern-day illustration, is a like a computer that's been programmed to give diagnostic checks. It's going to give a reading of where you are at. God gave you your conscience for this very purpose, so that you are able to take these readings in life and so make informed moral choices.

The conscience is 'programmed' to take its readings from God's moral law, the Ten Commandments. This point is well argued by Paul as he opens the epistle to the Romans. His argument there leads to this: that both Jews, who were born under the law, and Gentiles, who were born without the law, are equally guilty. He wrote in Romans 2:14–15, *For when gentiles who do not have the Law instinctively perform the requirements of the Law, these, though not having the Law, are a law to themselves, in that they show the work of the law **written in their hearts**, their conscience testifying . . .* (NASB).

All 'normal' people would agree that murder is wrong. This includes the atheist and agnostic. The Christian points to the

Bible as his source for this reckoning, the atheist doesn't know why he believes what he does but arrives at the same place. The law has already been written into his heart. Without realising it, his conscience is operating from the base of God's moral law written on his heart.

The big point of note is however, we as Christians are no longer under that law, a new law of love is now operating in our hearts. However, our conscience doesn't know this yet. It must be informed, renewed and transformed.

Someone said that life is a journey not a guided tour, but your conscience is the closest thing that you will get to a tour guide. It's there to help you relate with others and build meaningful relationships. Under the Holy Spirit's influence, your conscience will bring you to a point where you connect with God, walk with the Holy Spirit and make a difference in this world. We soon discover that God is a master at using imperfect people.

The Bible speaks of several 'grades' of conscience. There is such a thing as a good conscience, and Paul told Timothy to hold on to that for all its worth (1 Timothy 1:19). A good conscience is one that works well. This Greek word for good is *agathos*. It's more than just good in nature, but something that has its goodness originating in God and is **empowered** by Him in life. And there lies the key which we will come back to shortly.

The Bible also speaks about a defiled conscience. That is, the conscience has become so corrupted that it's no longer reliable or accurate; it's lost the ability to discern right from wrong. In extreme cases such people become sociopaths or even psychopaths. Doctors usually define these people as suffering from antisocial personality disorder.

Most experts believe psychopaths and sociopaths share a similar set of traits. Not only do they have a poor inner sense of right and wrong, but they don't seem to understand or share another person's feelings either, they have little or no empathy.

The Bible also speaks about a weak conscience. A person with a weak conscience may feel guilty when they haven't done anything wrong, but primarily a weak conscience is one that has no strength or vigour. Paul talks of such people in 1 Corinthians 8:7–13. In this case, there was a debate going on over the eating of meat from the markets that had first been offered to idols. Some said they could eat it, and others said don't touch it for it had become spiritually contaminated.

Paul uses the word *asthenes* to describe the weakness of conscience shown by those who wouldn't eat this meat, meaning their conscience is sick, feeble or impotent. Paul teaches if such people were to eat that meat, they would end up defiling their conscience, upsetting it, leaving a mark or blemish upon it. He concludes that they in that case would be better off not eating the meat and reminded those who were not in the least bothered by it to love, care and respect those who were troubled by it.

So, we could say that conscience is a relational tool, it's providing data that's designed to help us relate to God, each other and even to ourselves. In that you are a new creation, your conscience will now need re-educating, reprogramming. It needs a spiritual upgrade or else it will give you trouble. Learning how to deal with our own conscience is hugely important for a Christian, and sadly, many never get to that place. Hopefully we will today.

A few years ago, there was an almost fatal air accident at the OR Tambo International Airport in Johannesburg, South Africa. We were aware of it because we flew in with the same airline the very next day. An almost new Emirates Airbus took off for Dubai with a seasoned and skilled crew on board. This fully loaded aircraft struggled to gain altitude almost immediately as it lifted off the runway. The aircraft did not seem to have enough power to climb even though the engines were showing no fault. The pilots were perplexed as they struggled for more power. With seconds to spare they managed to bring the aircraft back under control to gain enough altitude to circle and do a go-round and land safely back at the airport. Apparently, upon review, the crew did not apply the correct protocol or procedure for take-off with their given parameters of weight and altitude. Consequently, the computers did not call for more power from the engines when they needed to climb, which almost ended in disaster.

Your conscience is like that. It is going to respond to two things, the information it receives and the way you then as a believer handle that information and direct your conscience. Sometimes, when our conscience is not functioning properly, it gives us a problem in our walk with God — we are not flying right, and some people unfortunately crash and burn.

Psychologists speak about a condition called cognitive dissonance. This is a condition that afflicts an individual when there is a conflict between what they believe in their heart of hearts and the way that they then try to behave. If there's a conflict between what they believe and what they try to do, there is a breakdown in that person's life. Sometimes it's a mental breakdown, sometimes it's behavioural patterns and oftentimes it's a spiritual crisis.

One Christian student recently said this to me as we were teaching a series on grace, 'I'm learning, but I can't make it stay in my head. It's already too different from what I had learned before. It seems too good to be true, so my brain keeps switching to default mode'. And default mode is more condemnation.

So, how can I stand before God without my heart condemning me?

No Condemnation. Not Now, Not Ever!

We ask all our Bible college students here at Destiny College to memorise Romans 8 by heart. Each year at a commissioning service we then get to hear the class recite it. I think that of all the wonderful texts in the Scriptures, Romans 8 has to be a shining light, a crown jewel in the Bible. There is enough in this one chapter to keep you going in your walk, your call and your destiny. It opens and begins with these words:

> *There is therefore now no condemnation*
> *to them which are in Christ Jesus.*
> **(ROMANS 8:1, KJV)**

Those using the KJV of the Bible might think that this is half the verse, for the 1611 KJV adds in the line *who walk not after the flesh but after the Spirit.* This is missing from newer translations because it wasn't there in the original Greek. Apparently, the 1611 translators could not believe that the opening phrase could stand on its own. It was too good to be true.

So, they repeated and added the phrase from the fourth verse. They thought that the only possibility of a 'no condemnation' scenario was if you 'walked' carefully in a particular fashion, thus giving no grounds for accusation. Only no sin or any sinful actions could possibly lead to the no condemnation status in their minds. But Paul has already pointed out that arriving at this new position of no condemnation has nothing at all, whatsoever, at any time, to do with your ability or condition. It is about your position or location. And that location is 'in Christ'. This error from the KJV is therefore corrected in newer translations.

When we look at the opening lines of Romans chapter eight, we read this word 'therefore', and often Bible teachers tell us that when we see the word 'therefore' in Scriptures, we should always ask 'what is it there for?' We realise that this phenomenal claim of 'no condemnation' is true because it's standing on all the truth previously explained in the earlier chapters, particularly the fifth chapter. In that fifth chapter we were told:

*But the free gift is not like the transgression. For if by the transgression of the one the many died, **much more** did the grace of God and the gift by the grace of the one Man, Jesus Christ, abound to the many.*

(ROMANS 5:15, NASB 1995)

Consequently, because of all that God did for us in Christ, there is now NO condemnation to those who are in Christ Jesus. It's very important to note that this is an absolute statement. It's full and final. Romans 8:1 could equally read, *there is therefore now, no, not now, not ever, or have any future possibility of there ever being, any* condemnation to those who are in Christ Jesus.

Not only is the Christian NOT in a state of condemnation, he never can be, not ever again. It is impossible for that to happen. The door has been well and truly shut. The justification by God of our lives through and because of our Lord Jesus Christ, is full, complete, final and eternal.

To be clear, the Christian is a person who can never be condemned. He may feel condemned and very aware that he's failed, but if his conscience his telling him that, then his conscience is out of date, misinformed and not telling him the **whole** truth. That conscience needs a download of a new upgrade.

The word 'no' in Romans 8:1 actually means 'never'. It is a very strong word. The apostle is asserting here that if we are Christians, our sins — past sins, present sins and future sins — have already been dealt with once and for all. Many of our troubles come down to a failure to realise the truth of that one verse. It's for this reason that the end of chapter eight, one of the most wonderful chapters in all the Bible, confirms that as a result there can never be any separation from the love of God.

No Condemnation — No Separation

Martin Luther spoke of learning to live between heaven and earth. By this, he meant bringing our conscience to a place where it is trained, taught and empowered by the gospel of grace to such a degree that when it accuses, it has little or no effect other than total gratitude and thanks from our hearts that we are forgiven and justified. Luther spoke of this as *proper spiritual gospel hearing*. He put it this way: '*Use that part of you that measures what God has against you and turn it now to hear that He has nothing against you*'. [17]

I love this comment from Dr Martyn Lloyd-Jones, one of the greatest theologians of the 20th century:

> *We must cease to think of ourselves merely as forgiven, merely as believers, merely holding onto Christ. The truth about us as Christians is that God by the Holy Spirit has put us into Christ, 'implanted' us 'in Him' — 'planted together'. So, you do not go in and out of that. You do not cease to be a Christian when you sin, you do not come under condemnation when you sin, you are not cast out of Christ when you sin. NO, you remain in Christ, and there is still no condemnation. You have sinned of course,*

but you have sinned against love and not against law. If
you have got a hold of this idea, you will have discovered
the most glorious truth you will ever know in your life. [18]

Here's the thing that many Christians don't get, God does not justify the righteous, He justifies the sinners, and that and therein lies the amazing gospel of astronomical grace. So, whilst we walk and often fail, we never fall from this new position. Some people have more confidence in the devil taking them than God keeping them. Billy Graham said this, *'It isn't your hold on God that saves you, it's His hold on you'.* [19]

Once Paul has explained in the most amazing way the radical gospel of grace and our justification by faith, he moves on to Romans 12 where he helps us understand how we can apply it. He writes:

Do not be conformed to this world, but be transformed by
the renewing of your mind, so that you may prove what the
will of God is, that which is good and acceptable and perfect.
(ROMANS 12:2, NASB)

Our minds, including our conscience, needs renewing, which means much more than a makeover. It means a constant process of renewal in line with gospel truth. This Greek word for 'renewing' is *anakainosis*, which means, among other things, 'a renewing or a renovation which makes a person different than in the past'. Not only do we need to know it, but we need to learn how to live there daily.

We said earlier that a 'good conscience' was one that firstly had its goodness originate in God, and secondly is sustained by God as it goes forward. A good conscience can only really be good if its inherent goodness originated in God in the first place, and since we are inherently sinful, that isn't possible. It's His righteousness. I need not mine.

Not only does a conscience accuse, it can excuse — *I didn't mean it, I'm no worse than anyone else, etc.* But a good conscience is not one which says, 'I haven't done anything wrong', but first and foremost says, 'He hasn't done anything wrong. He is perfectly right, and I am found in Him'.

God wants you to renew your conscience by His Word and forever live by faith in all that Christ has done. The devil, on the other hand, wants to remind your conscience (with the full weight of the law behind him) of all that you failed to do. **But even when you are wrong, you are right!** All our sins are already forgiven; we are already justified before God, and so our ongoing conversation is mostly filled with 'thank yous' more than 'sorrys', even when we fall short.

Like David of old we can say:

"Bring my soul out of prison,
So that I may give thanks to Your name;
The righteous will surround me,
For you will deal bountiful with me."
(PSALM 142:7, NASB 1995)

A Deep, Clean Conscience
and the Ashes of a Red Heifer

Here's an Old Testament concept explaining a fantastic New Testament truth:

> *The blood of goats and bulls and the ashes of a heifer*
> *sprinkled on those who are ceremonially unclean*
> *sanctify them so that they are outwardly clean.*
> *How much more, then, will the blood of Christ, who*
> *through the eternal Spirit offered himself unblemished*
> *to God, cleanse our consciences from acts that lead*
> *to death, so that we may serve the living God!*
> **(HEBREWS 9:13–14, NIV)**

Hebrews was written to Jewish converts, who under the pressure of heavy persecution were beginning to revert back to the Law, the Old Covenant and a religious lifestyle. It's author, who is unknown but possibly Paul, is telling them that this is a really bad idea, since what they now have in Christ is far superior in every way. Why would you want to go back to the law?

It's into this conversation that we are reminded about the ashes of a red heifer. So, what have the ashes of a red heifer got to do with you and your conscience today?

Let's begin in Romans 8, where we note that the Bible talks of two very different laws. One is identified as the 'law of the spirit of life in Christ' and the other as the 'law of sin and death'.

There is therefore now no condemnation for those who
are in Christ Jesus. For the law of the Spirit of life has set
you free in Christ Jesus from the law of sin and death.

(ROMANS 8:1–2, ESV)

Firstly, let me say that the Law as given through Moses is this law of sin and death mentioned here. Whilst some will argue otherwise, we clearly read of it defined as such in other places.

It's called the *ministry of death* (2 Corinthians 3:7), and we also read, *I was once alive apart from the Law; but when the commandment came, sin became alive and I died* (Romans 7:9, NASB 1995).

The Law can only ever call out sin, because that was its intention. And sin always leads to death, it's then seen as the law of sin and death. When pastors and preachers preach the law to the converted, they are preaching and proclaiming death to the hearers.

Sin is not only breaking or violating God's law, but sin is always a power and a pathway that leads to death. God is against death, He is a God of life, so God is against sin for the same reason. He doesn't want you to die. We think of death as ceasing to exist, *it's dead and gone.* But that's not the way the Bible sees or defines death. Death occurs when a person no longer exists in the form or condition God intended. God told Adam that Adam would die if he sinned. He sinned but lived another 900 years. However, His relationship with God was dead. His ability to exercise rule and dominion over the earth was dead. His dominion over sin and Satan was dead. Eventually his body followed suit.

The time came when God gave man the Law, but this Law, although good, has always been the law of sin and death. It cannot give man life, because just like Romans 8 said, the flesh does not possess the ability to keep the Law, so we are condemned and condemned to death. So, every contact with the Law can only bring despair, never hope.

Every time this law of sin and death touches us, it reminds us of our sins, and even the reminder of such kills. It kills our hope, our faith, our dreams. It can destroy our witness, it destroys our confidence, and above all, it destroys our relationship with God. The law always leaves us asking and wondering, 'How could God love me or even accept me?' When our conscience is in the grip of the law, it will always be in the grip of death at the same time.

But there is a greater law. This law of the spirit of life in Christ Jesus is greater and supersedes the other.

Gravity operates in every place on Planet Earth. We don't have a gravity free zone on Earth. The law of sin and death is the same, it operates everywhere regarding everyone all of the time. Yet we see birds and planes flying, overcoming the law of gravity. They do this by using a superior law, the law of aerodynamics and thrust. Such is the law of the spirit of life in Christ Jesus. The power of the latter is far superior to the former. Which brings us back to the ashes of a red heifer.

Maybe your Bible has a footnote in it at Hebrews 9:13, this will take you back to Numbers 19.

Here God instructs the people of Israel that touching anything dead will make you ceremonially unclean. Touch death and death will touch you. Not only was everyone who touched death defiled, but every *thing* that was touched by death was defiled also. If a man died in a tent, all persons in it and everything within it was defiled.

Not forgetting that everyone over the age of twenty was doomed to die in the wilderness (apart from Joshua and Caleb), death was everywhere all of the time as around half a million people died under judgement continuously over the next 40 years. This practice of touching no dead thing was far more than God's health and hygiene laws as some think, this was God showing how much sin, which leads to death, affects our lives.

You see, the Spirit of God is the Spirit of life. For the law of the spirit of life sets you free from the law of sin and death. Everything in God is vibrant. Everything in God is energised. Everything in God breaths, it's creative, it's passionate. It's exciting, it's over the top, it's always a more than enough life. This is the God that we serve, and this is the nature of His spirit. He is opposed to anything that's death or deathly or dead and dying.

Jesus came to give us life and life in all its fullness. And so, in the days in which these people lived, the reality of their lives meant that the moment they touched a dead relative, a friend, a neighbour, an animal — anything that was dead — they themselves were considered to be ceremonially unclean. To be ceremonially unclean meant they were just as dead in relationships and the religious life of the community. They were excluded and barred from everyday life.

God in His Grace made a provision that covered that eventuality. It worked like this. The priest had been instructed to take a red heifer and, unlike all the other sacrifices, was instructed to kill it and completely and totally incinerate every part of it. He was to be sure that this happened well outside the camp. This red heifer's ashes were taken to be added to the ashes of a scarlet thread, the ashes of a hyssop plant and the ashes of cedar wood. Then from this concoction they made a compound. This paste was to be placed and diligently kept outside their camp.

When any person became ceremonially defiled by touching death, they were instructed to come to the priest who would take them outside the camp, gather the ashes of the red heifer and mix those ashes with 'living' spring water (bubbling water), make a solution of it and sprinkle and splash the death-contaminated person. After this was done, they could once again stand clean and confidently say that the power of death has died to them. They were now clean and free to get on with their life.

It's interesting how many comparisons there are in this story which is a type and a shadow of the gospel of grace. The Bible says that Jesus, just like the red heifer, was taken outside the camp to be killed on Calvary's hill. Some Jewish theologians say that when the priest was choosing the red heifer for this sacrifice and function that even if he found just two black hairs on it, he would disqualify that red heifer. Jesus was sinless in every way, and tried at a court not once but twice, and Pilate said, *I find no fault in this man* (Luke 23:4, KJV). Furthermore, Adam's name means 'red' or 'red earth'. That red heifer was standing in for Adam's children until Jesus came, who Paul calls the last Adam (not the second Adam since we will never ever need a third Adam.)

Hyssop is a plant that has a beautiful fragrance, so implying that the red heifer's compound and mixture would remove from the contaminated person the stench of death and add the sweet fragrance of life. The scarlet thread, of course, speaks of the precious blood of Jesus shed for us once and for all for the complete and total forgiveness of sins. The cedar wood which speaks of both strength and prosperity in Scripture. Can you see just how complete we are in Christ?

Unlike other sacrifices and offerings in Old Testament times, this red heifer application and sacrifice was entirely free, somebody else had paid for it. In other words, all the stench of death was taken from them freely; it was a free gift. The people could come and take of it as often as they wished — no set limits, no quotas, no expiration date.

When your conscience is speaking death to you and it's reminding you of your moral failures, faults and weaknesses, you have something better than the ashes of a red heifer. Just as they went to the ashes of a red heifer, you can confidently come through the eternal spirit to our Lord and Saviour Jesus Christ and say, 'I'm cleansed, liberated and accepted. The loudest voice in my life is not going to be the voice of my conscience, but the voice of the Spirit'.

Unlike the ashes of the red heifer, the blood of Jesus performs a permanent cleansing process, so why should we spend one moment of one day lost in regret or depression? The story of the red heifer tells us that God hasn't reluctantly cleansed and forgiven us, but fully, completely and lavishly. We are cleansed, strengthened, restored and even smelling great! It's time to inform our conscience of this truth.

Remember when John spoke about Jesus? In John's Gospel it says, *". . . we beheld His glory, the glory as of the only begotten of the Father, full of grace and truth"* (John 1:14, NKJV). John says the law came through Moses, but grace and truth came through Jesus. Whose side is truth on? The law or grace? Grace is the correct answer.

We read earlier in 1 John 3:21 (NASB) which says *"Beloved, if our heart does not condemn us, we have confidence before God."* But let me show you 1 John 3:19–20:

> *"We will know by this that we are of the truth,*
> *and will assure our heart before Him in whatever*
> *our heart condemns us; for God is greater*
> *than our heart, and knows all things."*
>
> **(NASB 1995)**

Do you think God is ignorant of what you did? He knows all things. But what does it say? *"We will know by this that we are of the truth, and we will assure our heart before Him in whatever our heart condemns us."* Does your heart flash up a memory of something you've done wrong? Does your heart flash up a memory of something that was done to you? Does your heart flash up a memory and say, *This was done to you, but it was your fault, you asked for it?*

Too many people have been victims of some form of sexual abuse, and amongst these there are those who actually believe it was in some way their own fault, so they are the ones who feel profoundly guilty, and so they stay silent for years.

We all have a choice to make. Are we going to come to God on the basis of law or grace?

Good counselling can often help people move forwards, but there is nothing like grace-filled truth to set you free.

"We will know by this that we are of the truth, and will assure our heart before Him in whatever our heart condemns us."

How do you think Paul the Apostle felt many years later when he recollected that he stood by and watched the murderous stoning of the evangelist Steven? Paul guarded the coats and the bags of those who killed Steven, being the official witness to the fact. As the witness, he would have certified Steven's death as his battered, bloody body lay on the ground.

The Bible says Paul went into houses harassing whole families. We read that *Saul, still breathing threats and murder against the disciples of the Lord* (Acts 9:1, NKJV), carried many others off to prison. It goes on to say *". . . so that if he found any belonging to the Way, whether men or women, he might bring them bound to Jerusalem"* (Acts 9:2, NKJV). Don't you think Paul should have had a problem with his conscience till the day he died?

But he didn't. He did refer to himself as the chief of sinners (1 Timothy 1:15). But he understood, even if his heart brought up a flashback of something he did, he could throw his hands up and say 'guilty' but throw his head up and say 'righteous'. Paul understood this. He even said things like this:

But to me it is an insignificant matter that I
would be examined by you, or by any human
court; in fact, I do not even examine myself.

(1 CORINTHIANS 4:3, NASB)

Most of us spend our days scrutinising our performance,
analysing ourselves.

'If you live by self-analyses, you will die by self-analyses'.

MARTIN LUTHER

John said, *Beloved, if our heart does not condemn us, we have*
confidence before God (1 John 3:21, NASB). He wasn't saying your
heart doesn't condemn you because you haven't done anything
wrong. He was saying your heart doesn't condemn you because
you've come to realise that in Christ there is no condemnation,
and all of this is by grace.

Notice that the writer of Hebrews said that the outcome of
such a place was intended so that we can serve God — the **living**
God — with all His power, wisdom and might flowing through us.

The blood of goats and bulls and the ashes of a heifer
sprinkled on those who are ceremonially unclean
sanctify them so that they are outwardly clean.
How much more, then, will the blood of Christ, who

*through the eternal Spirit offered himself unblemished
to God, cleanse our consciences from acts that lead
to death, so that we may serve the living God!*

(HEBREWS 9:13–14, NIV)

We need to remind ourselves of one last point. The ashes of this red heifer were to be mixed with living water, or literally 'bubbling water'. This water either had to be taken from a fresh flowing spring, or from water collected directly from heaven — not stored, not filtered, not touched by human hands. This was the water Jesus offered the woman at the well in John 4; this was the water Jesus spoke of as He shouted out on the great day of the feast in John 7; this was the water poured out from heaven at Pentecost; this is the eternal Spirit of God, now designated to live and move in your heart, a heart free from condemnation.

Stand up, step out, start believing.

*'Lay aside your sackcloth and ashes, and rise to the dignity
of your new position; you are little in Israel because you
will be so, not because there is any necessity for it'.* [20]

C.H. SPURGEON

7

The Kingdom of God and the Life of Grace

God was at the centre of my theology,
but I was at the centre of my life.

UNKNOWN

For many people, an awakening to grace can be shocking, alarming, and yet totally liberating. But it's so often not the gospel that they were first introduced to or are familiar with in their church experience. Therefore, when it comes to the questions about the gospel of grace, many people say — and I have heard it from pastors in particular — that their biggest concern is morality and behaviour. If the law is not taught, they think, how will Christians know how to behave and conduct themselves? They fear that we will be left with chaos in our churches, immorality in our lives and the evils of licentiousness undermining our testimonies. All of us of course are naturally concerned about these very important questions on the Christian's life, discipleship, growth and maturity, but this line of thinking suggests that there is a very low view of genuine Christianity.

Regrettably, where we find legalism, we find just as many moral failures amongst its leaders, and it's often the case that young people end up living secret lives being afraid to share their challenges, and then consequently being buried under condemnation and judgement, leave the church (or worse) and give up altogether. Sadly, we the pastors have sometimes been the worst at it in our own homes, and there are a whole generation of PKs (pastor's kids) out there hurting.

This thinking assumes that the law is the means God uses as the power source for transformational living in the life of the believer. Yet Paul wrote to tell us that he was not ashamed of the gospel (Romans 1:16), which was an understated way of actually saying that he was wild about it. He made a huge claim (inspired by the Holy Spirit) that this gospel was in fact the power of God unto salvation. Salvation means being made whole in every way, a transformed life in other words, not just a ticket to heaven.

Others fear that we will end up with that age-old heresy of antinomianism, which in itself had wide and varying views but essentially means 'law haters' or 'against the law'. They accused the apostle Paul of such a view in his day, but it was an accusation he refuted robustly. They had misunderstood his preaching of the gospel to be anti-Moses and anti-law. He sounded to them as if he was determined to throw out all his history and his heritage. Paul was never against the Law, but he understood its role, place and limitations. More importantly, he understood the power of the gospel and was so very grateful for its liberating reality.

Then there are other Christians who believe that the whole point of being born again is to arrive at the place where you can live by and live out the Law. To them this fulfils the biblical command *"Be holy, because I am holy"* (Leviticus 11:45, NIV). They teach that the Holy Spirit within empowers one for a new law-living life without. In other words, a sin-free, law-living life is within reach and striking distance, which in turn becomes their target objective. Perhaps even without realising it, they are setting out to serve the law and its demands. Various holiness movements have arisen around this idea over the years.

Some others also reason that since Jesus kept the law in every point, so should we. After all, don't we want to be like Jesus? He's our role model, right?

Others go even further and argue that we should see the positive side of the law in this respect: It's the rulebook for this game called life, and if we want to win at life, we should play by these rules. In fact, we should be found loving the moral law of God, for it leads to successful living.

Whilst sounding so plausible, these things clearly, are NOT the teaching of the New Testament. Far from it. So, what does the Bible say about this? I often tell our emerging leaders at Destiny College that there are several very important distinctions between secular leadership and spiritual leadership. Here's the first one: spiritual leaders recognize that . . .

#1 *Our knowledge source is different*
We believe the Bible to be God's infallible Word. It is our final authority on all matters.

Our knowledge source is not primarily the universities, philosophers, media, our church traditions, denomination, favourite theologians, other religions or popular culture. It's God's Word. What does it actually say on this subject?

On this subject of law and grace, we are left in absolutely no doubt; we are told that we are dead to the law.

> *Therefore, my brethren, you also were made to die to the Law through the body of Christ, so that you might be joined to another, to Him who was raised from the dead, in order that we might bear fruit for God.*
> (ROMANS 7:4, NASB 1995)

> *"For through the Law I died to the Law, so that I might live to God."*
> (GALATIANS 2:19, NASB)

The picture Paul paints in Romans is of a marriage. It's a terrible marriage, where the husband is a perfectionist fault finder; nothing is ever good enough as far as he is concerned. We might well know couples like that, and such marriages are never pleasant to be around — a constant flow of criticism, a harsh tongue and stern looks. The husband is never pleased and always irritated. Sometimes it's the other way around. It's the wife who gives a never-ending flow of corrective comment, often on trivial things in a conversation, so the husband chooses to live in the garden shed or the golf course.

The motive for these harsh actions is the need to 'be right', and that's exactly what legalism is and does. It presses home the need to be 'right' by telling yourself or others you are 'wrong'. That is the language and vocabulary of legalism. It kills churches, fellowship and families. It's constantly calling you out with 'you don't do it this way; you must do it that way'. Where 'it' can be any myriad of things in church and life.

I once had a lady come up to me at the end of a meeting and very irately say, 'It's awful. I think it's terrible'. I had no idea what she was talking about, so she made it clear. She was upset at the 20 or 30 people who were standing outside the church door smoking before they came into the service. I explained that our new Scottish laws now forbid smoking in public venues and they were no longer allowed to smoke in the building. Well, that made it worse. I heard, 'That's not what I mean, and you know it'. I found myself saying, 'Lady, smoking is the least of their problems. They have bigger things to deal with, and I'm sure God will get around to their smoking at some point'. She left the church and never came back; she had more anger over their smoking and me allowing it to continue at the church front door than joy that sinners were coming to church and finding Christ.

But then Paul goes on to say: That was you; you were that married person, married to that fault-finding law. However, a great event has happened. There has been a death, and consequently, you are free from such a marriage. The jurisdiction of such a partner has ended as far as you are concerned, and all involved are relieved. I once read an epitaph on a gravestone which said,

So here lies my wife, now let her lie.
She's at rest and so am I.

We are meant to be at rest from our fault-finding partner, but here's the point: It's not the law that died — it is still very much alive and well — it's you and I that died. That's how we get free from the law.

Why then would you want to renew a relationship with the law? Especially when Paul continues with his analogy and says we have now found a new partner in this new life. We have been joined or 'married' to another — Christ! So, if we go back to renew a relationship with our old partner (the law), we are actually being unfaithful to our new partner, Jesus. We call that adultery.

Law and grace should not co-exist in the one individual, but all too often they do. They cannot effectively walk together in that they are pulling in different directions. They can't be running mates. You really must choose one or the other. In fact, as we have already said in an earlier chapter, the purpose of the law was to lead you to grace.

You may ask, when exactly did we die? We died the moment we came to Christ; we were crucified with Him on the cross. I am both dead to and free from the law. Isn't that good news?

We are reminded of this in the lines from Augustus Toplady's wonderful hymn 'A Debtor to Mercy Alone':

A debtor to mercy alone,
Of covenant mercy I sing,
Nor fear, with God's righteousness on,
My person and off'rings to bring.
The terrors of law and of God
With me can have nothing to do;
My Savior's obedience and blood
Hide all my transgressions from view.

The second difference between spiritual leadership and secular leadership is this: Spiritual leaders realise . . .

#2 *We are here to serve a name, not make one*
We're not here to make a name for ourselves or to build our company or ministry brand. Building a brand is fully acceptable and expected in the world order of things, but not in this new life, this kingdom life. It may be right in the marketplace but not here, not now in our lives.

We're now here in this wonderful new relationship to serve the name of Jesus and make Him famous. Or in other words, to glorify God in all that we do. And that is the essential key for right living.

This chapter's opening quote is so often true. It is very possible to have God at the centre of our theology, but we are at the centre of our own lives. God's will or His ways don't get a look in.

It's possible to be theologically correct in all you believe, yet at the same time miss the point of being a Christian entirely. There are more modern Pharisees around than we would care to admit. The Pharisee was always concerned about being right, and then seen to be the one that was right. The Pharisee's speciality was to look down with disdain on those who couldn't muster his level of law-living discipline or were not as accurate with law interpretation as he so loved to be. He became very good at the moral lecture. You don't have to look far for these people; they are all over YouTube lecturing other ministries and pastors on their faults and failures.

I once took issue with a very successful and well-known preacher. He was busy posting on YouTube his dismissal of the character and theology of other equally well-known preachers. It wasn't that his theology was wrong, but his practice was entirely. I appealed to him that at the very least he should speak with these people personally. He hadn't once personally spoken to any of these people he so loved character assassinating. In his opinion, he was right and they were wrong, and he wanted the world to know. Unfortunately, he was found wanting not long after that, and his large ministry fell apart. An old pastor used to say, *'You will get further with the oil can of grace than the sword of accusation'*. And I for one, have been grateful for several ministry mentors, leaders and brothers who have challenged me in my life and its journey on occasions. The potential pitfall is that we can be that Pharisee and not even know it. No doubt, there is some Pharisee in all of us, that is why we all need grace so desperately.

Grace is risky; it will take you where others don't want you to go. It may well move you out beyond the four walls of Christian respectability. I'm not talking of good sound protocol and etiquette that should be part and parcel of any Christian's life. Billy

Graham made it to the end of a long and effective ministry life without moral failures or scandals, at least in part because of the personal protocol he always followed. We teach our developing leaders early on the dangers of the 'three Gs', which are gold, glitter and girls/guys. I still won't take a lady other than my wife or family into a car with me on her own. If you want a ride, bring a friend, or I'll pay for your cab. If there is a fall likely, it will always be in one of those three areas.

But on this 'risky grace' life, Jesus is our role model. On so many occasions, He was derided because He was friends with 'tax collectors and sinners'. We can so quickly think of the woman at the well, the seductress who had been with six different men already. Her life changed that day for sure, even though the disciples were shell-shocked to find Jesus speaking with her when they returned. What about the women caught in the very act of adultery? What was she wearing as she was thrown down before Jesus? Do you think that her legalistic accusers would give her time to get properly dressed?

Then remember the insane, ranting demoniac, bound to be every deacon's nightmare. Or the stinking lepers that no one would want to sit next to in church. Or the very wealthy but hated Zacchaeus, who was the conversation point of angry gossip many a night?

We so often sanitize our Bibles, making all the stories respectable but miss the blatantly obvious human details. However, grace boldly goes where religion fears to tread. If being seen to keep the moral law is the most important thing in your life, you won't want to go anywhere near those who fail at that miserably.

When the fullness of the grace of God changes your heart, it will not leave you in your comfort zones.

Sometimes, it's those around you that press this respectability button the most, usually because they have a vested interest in maintaining your position or success. They ask you, 'What will people think?' or they'll say, 'You can't be seen to respond like that'. That's what Michal did to her husband King David when he danced before the Lord. Rebuking David for his un-kingly behaviour, David essentially replied, *'You haven't seen anything yet'*. David went on to become a great King; Michal was childless all her days.

In the Parable of the Prodigal Son, this was also the problem the elder brother had with his father. It was not 'dignified' to accept a prostitute-loving, money-wasting son back home. *We are a 'respectable' family.*

But such a person is a contradiction of Christianity, a living, walking oxymoron, a contradiction in terms. That's why the religious, law-living class clashed with Jesus so often. Like others have said before me, *'No one cares how much you know until they know how much you care'.*

One time a journalist in a large national newspaper wrote a story about me and our ministry and called me the leader and founder of a 'fundamentalist sect'. Clearly the reporter did not know what either was, he just tried to find words that sounded as scandalous and as derogatory as possible. I had to laugh, since a fundamentalist is one who will stay totally committed to an already established body of truth, and a sect is a group that has diverted from it — making us an oxymoron, a contradiction in terms. I couldn't be both at the same time. Yet many of our Christian family think they are pleasing God by fighting for doctrinal purity and moral high ground whilst making life unbearable for everyone around them, including their own families. Often times such an emphasis in a church produces few new converts and drives away young people. Sinners loved Jesus, yet he was the holiest human who ever walked the planet.

And here's the thing, holiness does not mean being without fault or being sin free, although Jesus clearly was. Holiness is the hallmark of a dedicated life, given over for a cause, set apart, here to glorify God. You can keep all the commandments and yet still be the most unholy person around. Paul claimed he kept the law faultlessly, yet when Jesus appeared to him on that Damascus Road, Paul was asked, *"Why are you persecuting me?"* (Acts 9:4, NKJV). Paul had been thinking he was living a holy, law-living life, when in fact he was living as an anti-Christ!

The Christian life is a much higher calling than the law-living, law-keeping life. We as Christians should get to the place where we stop being concerned with 'being right' or being seen to be 'right'. The quest for holiness is not the quest for perfection, but the quest for no question — God first, last and always.

We should aim to say as Jim Elliot of old,

'One treasure, a single eye, and a sole Master'. [21]

It's not that 'right' no longer matters, but our place, grounding and foundation of being right has changed. It's no longer us earning it, learning it or proving it. It's 'being' it, which can only come by being justified by God and then secure enough to enjoy it and live in the good of that.

This new life goes much further. It's a grace-filled, grace-energised life. It's a life lived beyond living by the rules; it's life lived for a cause, His cause and His kingdom. We are all in ministry, it's just that for a minority of us, it happens to be in the church. Where do you minister? At home? In the marketplace? In law enforcement? In a school or a hospital? In your neighbourhood? You can minister anytime, anywhere.

Living by the law is like being an accountant: measuring costs, metering things out to the penny, going so far but no further, doing your dues, keeping your responsibilities. It's just like the elder brother in the Prodigal Son parable, who complained when his lost brother came home. It wasn't fair, couldn't be right. Dad threw the prodigal a party when he just didn't deserve it. He, the elder son, had behaved in a morally acceptable way, and what did he get? He may have said, '*So, let that son of yours sleep in the cowshed until he's earned his space and earned his place if he has to be here at all*'.

The implication in this story is that the elder brother was serving his father for earned reward and not for heartfelt love, so he was the true prodigal in the story, far away from His father's heart, and resenting all of it. It seems to me that too many Christians are leaving churches because of the same kind of resentment as found in this elder brother. They resent having to serve, or at least serve in the way asked or expected, they resent new people coming in and taking their place or position. They resent it when things change, and the church wishes or wants to move forwards. If we lose sight of love and grace and live by legalisms and laws, we could so easily end up in the same place. We don't have to serve; we GET to serve the King of Kings. Isn't that the greatest of all privileges?

Or it's like another parable Jesus told of a landowner hiring daily workers. He offers a penny for a day's work and they agree. Later that morning, he finds others standing on the street corners, and he hire's them at the same rate. Later still, almost at the end of the day, he hires yet more for the same daily rate. When time came for payment, those who worked the whole day in the hot heat of the sun were upset that they got the same pay as the last ones in. They also thought it unfair: *Doesn't the law have something to say about this? I deserve more.* The law will always make you go one way or the other: either I deserve it, or I don't deserve it.

Yet they in this parable got everything they agreed to, so why complain if the landowner wishes to be generous with others?

The law-living life doesn't know largesse or generosity, it only knows how to keep precise amounts, tallies and totals, lists of wrongs done and favours owed. It's competitive and critical, judgemental and judicial. The exact opposite of the famous love written about in 1 Corinthians 13. Take a moment and read that chapter reminding yourself of what a grace walk looks like.

The essence of Christianity is the Lordship of Christ. We are not saved by accepting Jesus as saviour but accepting Jesus as Lord. At which point He becomes our saviour. He can't save you unless you absolutely place all of your life in His hands.

If you openly declare that Jesus is Lord and believe in your heart that God raised him from the dead, you will be saved.

(ROMANS 10:9, NLT)

In other words, all of these things we have said point us to a completely different place. They point us in an entirely new direction from law-living. Something far bigger and vastly superior, they point us into **the kingdom of God**. We have now become citizens of an altogether different kingdom, which does life very differently than anything we have known before.

In comparison to the kingdom, law-living is the low life.

The Kingdom of God

For He rescued us from the domain of darkness, and transferred us to the kingdom of His beloved Son.

(COLOSSIANS 1:13, NASB)

I live in the UK — the United Kingdom — whose head of state is the Queen. It's a kingdom with a monarchy. Her presence touches everything important. Our government goes under the title H.M. Government. That is, Her Majesty's Government. When we have the annual state opening of parliament for a new sitting, our Queen will give the Queen's speech, within which she will always refer to 'my government,' and then tell of what they intend to do in the coming parliamentary year.

The names of our navy's battle ships are always prefixed HMS, which means 'Her Majesty's Ships'. All serving police officers have her crown on their hats, helmets and on their lapels, for they serve under the crown. Even the UK's finances are overseen by the H.M. Treasury.

On becoming a Christian, a marvellous thing happens. We are taken from one kingdom and transferred into another. We leave the kingdom of darkness, and we enter the kingdom of God.

We have to be born into this new kingdom. Born first into the world, born again into the kingdom of God. This kingdom has a King, and His name is Jesus. And unlike our UK monarch — who whilst having a great deal of love and respect, has very little real power on her throne since Oliver Cromwell — our King is all-powerful. This is the name I honour, love and serve. His name should be on everything I am or own, including my gifts and talents. H.M. Andrew Owen. *His Majesty's Servant*. And when I consider how much He has done for me, I find myself saying, just like Paul:

> *"I have been crucified with Christ; and it is no longer*
> *I who live, but Christ lives in me; and the life which*
> *I now live in the flesh I live by faith in the Son of*
> *God, who loved me and gave Himself up for me."*
> **(GALATIANS 2:20, NASB)**

Not only have I died to the law, I've died to myself. I have died both to my wrongs and to any rights. I'm called to live out this kingdom life, which doesn't even compute living the same way as the law-lived life. That's why Paul had to write in Romans 12, reminding those early believers that even the way we think about things has to change.

> *And do not be conformed to this world, but be*
> *transformed by the renewing of your mind, so*
> *that you may prove what the will of God is, that*
> *which is good and acceptable and perfect.*
> (ROMANS 12:2, NASB)

This is Paul's instruction on Christian behaviour transformed, he told us, by the renewing of our minds. No appeal to the big ten — the Ten Commandments — there.

I'm sure that you must have heard a sermon sometime telling you that this word 'transformed' in the original Greek is *metamorphoó*, from which we get our English word 'metamorphosis'. Kingdom life should so transform our lives that we don't look anything like our former 'caterpillar' selves, crawling along under the cabbage leaves of life. The law could never do such a thing, change us like that! Yet some Christians are like the two caterpillars talking with each other under a cabbage leaf as a butterfly passes over head. One caterpillar says to the other, *'You will never get me up in one of those things'*. And sadly, that is how they see grace, something best avoided, not realising they were born to fly.

We mentioned earlier in this book of an issue that arose in the church at Rome. One faction of the church said that they must not eat any meat offered to idols, and another faction argued back saying, *What's wrong with you? It's just meat.* I used the point earlier to talk about conscience, but there was actually something much more important going on here. These Roman Christians were forgetting who they were — kingdom people. So, Paul wrote and said:

> *For the kingdom of God is not a matter of*
> *eating and drinking, but of righteousness,*
> *peace and joy in the Holy Spirit.*
> **(ROMANS 14:17, NIV)**

They were reverting to law-living, reducing their lives to rules about things. The two factions were judging the other, claiming each side was wrong, and each side was claiming they were right. One side was called too legalistic and the other side called too liberal. No doubt they had probably appealed to Paul to tell them which side was right and asked what rules to apply in this situation. Paul reminds them it's not about rules and not to be petty, but to be large-hearted, gracious, preferring one another. Make space for grace.

Paul was at pains to point out that the kingdom of God wasn't concerned with such things as food and drink, but it was deeply concerned about their responses to one another in the heat of that moment. Where was the peace and the joy? This kingdom, said Paul, was concerned with the matters of righteousness, peace and joy, and all of it lived in the Holy Spirit.

The law reverts to morals and morality, but the kingdom of God reverts to righteousness. Morality asks is it black or white, right or wrong. What do the rules say? The morality rule of the law said that the women caught in adultery should be stoned to death, but the higher 'law' of righteousness said she could and should be saved. Righteousness is not only a condition within which God stands, but an application by which God acts. Righteousness trumps morality every time. God has both given us that same righteousness and told us to seek it out every time, every place, everywhere.

> *Seek first the kingdom of God and His righteousness . . .*
> **(MATTHEW 6:33, NKJV)**

Righteousness doesn't only ask what is right or wrong, or even ask *who* is right or wrong, but asks how should I act and respond in this situation? How would grace respond? How would God respond to me? Let me put it this way, God in grace is always looking for the redemptive approach, that's what grace does. Grace is never politically guided, looking for the popular or expedient way out, but often choses the most costly and inconvenient way forward. Unlike the law, which only wants to condemn, grace wants to redeem every last soul.

When Adam sinned, God didn't throw him away. He didn't discard him and start again. He promised Satan, in Adam's hearing, that He would restore and renew through another Adam, a last Adam that would one day come. And so, the famous Genesis 3:15 was proclaimed, now loved and known by theologians as the *protoevangelium*, the first proclamation of the gospel.

The Kingdom Life and Your Identity

As we opened this chapter, we made reference to those who sometimes struggle to understand the relationship between some things Jesus did and what we must now do. I have heard preachers say that Jesus kept the law in every point, He made it His business to do that, and therefore, we His followers must be prepared to do the same. They revert to this passage:

> *"Do not think that I have come to abolish the Law or the Prophets; I have not come to abolish them but to fulfil them. For truly I tell you, until heaven and earth disappear, not the smallest letter, not the least stroke of a pen, will by any means disappear from the Law until everything is accomplished. Therefore anyone who sets aside one of the least of these commands and teaches others accordingly will be called least in the kingdom of heaven, but whoever practices and teaches these commands will be called great in the kingdom of heaven. For I tell you that unless your righteousness surpasses that of the Pharisees and the teachers of the law, you will certainly not enter the kingdom of heaven.*
>
> (MATTHEW 5:17–20, NIV)

These verses in Matthew 5 are so important when we are speaking of the kingdom, our identity and behaviour — they are crucial to our understanding.

Firstly, we read that Jesus said He came to do something that we could **never** do. He said that He had come to **fulfil** the law.

The essential message of Christianity tells us that this is beyond our ability, so Jesus came to do some things we must freely admit we cannot do, and so we rest in His work not ours. We gladly and gratefully remember that He went on to say, '*It is finished*', job done! Since that task is successfully completed, I am not required to attempt again to fulfil the law.

I love the way the Message says this:

> *"Don't suppose for a minute that I have come to demolish*
> *the Scriptures — either God's Law or the Prophets.*
> *I'm not here to demolish but to complete. I am going to put*
> *it all together, pull it all together in a vast panorama."*
> **(MATTHEW 5:17, MSG)**

That vast new panorama is the kingdom of God.

In Matthew 5, Jesus seems to toughen up the stance of the law by warning against the setting aside of even the smallest part of this law, famously written as *jot or tittle* in older translations of the Bible. This was making reference to the smallest letter in the Greek alphabet and smallest stroke of the pen, implying the tiniest detail of the Law was as important as its headlines. In other words, if you were going to set out to live by this Law, make sure you complete ALL of it, for just a small failure in part is failure in the whole.

But yet more, Jesus was pointing towards a quality of life that will mean living *beyond* these things; it does better, superseding the righteousness of the Pharisees.

As the chapter progresses, Jesus goes on to talk not just about the law's take on murder, but the kingdom's take on murder. He said that anger in your heart is a killer, and lust in your life leads to imaginary adultery, which in kingdom thinking is as good as doing it! Thought is ancestor to the deed! The law focuses on external practices, but now the kingdom is working on internal processes. Then, we are told by Jesus, that our righteousness must surpass the righteousness of the Pharisees and teachers of the day. Bearing in mind that they had created and identified 613 laws which were added to the Ten Commandments. How can our righteousness surpass theirs? There is only one possibility: We need a different kind of righteousness, God's own righteousness.

Here's the big deal, we are not called to 'copy' Jesus. He is not simply our role model. It's not about us being like Jesus. Do we actually think that we can copy Jesus Christ and do what He did? The truth is that a Christian is not one who tries to impersonate Jesus, but lets the real Jesus into their hearts and allows Him to live through them. The kingdom of God is here because the King of this kingdom is within you and me.

Neither shall they say, Lo here! or, lo there!
for, behold, the kingdom of God is within you.
(LUKE 17:21, KJV)

The first big step a new believer in Christ is instructed to take is water baptism, and there is no doubt that biblically that should be by full immersion. But why is that so important? Why does Romans 6 tell us it's a very important foundation to our Christian lives? Well, it's going to be the only way we can possibly live this kingdom life. We die, and dead people get buried. Buried in the waters of baptism.

This life is a new kingdom life. And in this life, the Holy Spirit is assisting us. Not by applying the law or convicting us of sin as we have already said, but first by being sure we know that we're dead and giving us a proper burial in baptism. Then raising us up into newness of life by the indwelling power of His Holy Spirit and applying the fertilizer of grace so that good fruit grows.

> *To them God has chosen to make known among*
> *the Gentiles the glorious riches of this mystery,*
> *which is Christ in you, the hope of glory.*
> **(COLOSSIANS 1:27, NIV)**

The Beatitudes

If there was any one piece of New Testament writings that could supersede Exodus 20 and the law, it would have to be Matthew 5 and the famous Sermon on the Mount, which included the Beatitudes and the Lord's Prayer. Within Exodus 20, we have Moses' rules for life, and a very severe warning: *Don't come near or touch this mountain.* Whilst within the latter, we have Jesus' manifesto for His kingdom life and an invitation, not a warning — an invitation to come near. You can do so by praying, and when you pray, start your prayers by saying *"Our Father in heaven . . ."* One is not only far superior to the other, the one calls out failure before we start, the other calls out hope to the desperately underserving.

Of the two, however, there is probably more familiarity with the Ten Commandments than the Beatitudes. Kurt Vonnegut illustrates this idea in *Man Without A Country.* In this work, Vonnegut takes on politics, American society and religion. Vonnegut correctly refers to the numerous politicians that use the media to call for the Ten Commandments to be posted at the courthouse or at city hall. The most vocal Christians, however, rarely call for the same treatment of the Beatitudes. This may be understandable in that the Bible tells us that the law was given to and for the law breaker.

We also know that the law is made not for the righteous but for lawbreakers and rebels, the ungodly and sinful, the unholy and irreligious, for those who kill their fathers or mothers, for murderers.
(1 TIMOTHY 1:9, NIV)

It's interesting when you compare the Ten Commandments with the Beatitudes. The law opens with a threat, *"Thou shalt not . . ."* but the Beatitudes open with a blessing, *"Blessed are . . ."*

Here they are:

"Blessed are the poor in spirit, for theirs
is the kingdom of heaven.
Blessed are those who mourn, for they shall be comforted.
Blessed are the meek, for they shall inherit the earth.
Blessed are those who hunger and thirst for
righteousness, for they shall be filled.
Blessed are the merciful, for they shall obtain mercy.
Blessed are the pure in heart, for they shall see God.
Blessed are the peacemakers, for they
shall be called sons of God.
Blessed are those who are persecuted for righteousness'
sake, for theirs is the kingdom of heaven.
(MATTHEW 5:3–10, NKJV)

In my mind, these statements said by Jesus sum up the new kingdom order; it's a pathway to grace and grace-filled living. I see these kingdom-living statements as having a far more profound effect on a person's life than the Ten Commandments. These things will not only change your behaviour, they will change your nature. Many books have been written on this subject, with some authors calling them the 'be happy attitudes'. So many politicians promise to change human conditions, but only Jesus can change human nature.

In continuing my advice to our Destiny College students on the differences between spiritual leadership and secular leadership, it brings us to the third difference between spiritual leadership and secular leadership . . .

#3. Our power source is different

Thousands of books have been written on 'self-confidence', including some Christian books, yet these two words never occur together in the entire Bible. Not once! Self-confidence is not a kingdom concept. In fact, confidence in yourself is a real bad idea.

But we often read of things like *'your confidence'*:

> *So do not throw away your confidence;*
> *it will be richly rewarded.*
> **(HEBREWS 10:35, NIV)**

Or in the New Living Translation:

> *So do not throw away this confident trust in the Lord.*
> *Remember the great reward it brings you!*
> **(HEBREWS 10:35, NLT)**

Secular leaders brim over with, and take time to develop, their self-confidence, but spiritual leaders have something better — God-confidence — an unswerving trust in a God who is always faithful.

Grace is the conduit to unmerited favour for divine help, strength and provision. That's why I personally think that the greatest promise God ever made to us was that He will never leave us nor forsake us (Deuteronomy 31:6). He is our power source. Grace is in relentless pursuit of a human-divine relationship, knowing that this relationship can only be sustained by the divine input. The challenge is getting the human input to realise that. That's where the Beatitudes come in, they walk us to that place. Let's take a look and see how.

Firstly, I think it's worth noting that the Sermon on the Mount was intended to be seen in direct comparison with Moses who received the Law on Mount Sinai. Why don't we call it the *Sermon in the Meadow* or the *Preach in the Park?* It's called the Sermon on the Mount for the reason it took place on a mountain, although unnamed. Jesus is contrasted by John when he wrote and said, *"For the law was given through Moses; grace and truth came through Jesus Christ"* (John 1:17, NIV). One greater than Moses has arrived, and what He's bringing on this mountain is far better news than that which was brought by Moses on that mountain.

Blessed are the poor in spirit, for theirs is the kingdom of heaven. Poor in spirit is not the same as being money or asset poor. The Greek word used for poor is *ptóchos,* and literally means 'cringing beggar', a person who's gone beyond poor, he is at the very end of himself, nothing left, the utter helplessness that comes with such a position. But only when we come to the very end of ourselves can we come to the new dawn of the kingdom life. We've given up trying and are now so grateful for grace. Our end is God's opportunity to get started.

The law says try harder, whilst grace says stop trying! It's time to start receiving. The beggar is welcomed in and given the right clothes for the banquet. The righteousness of Jesus Christ.

Blessed are those who mourn, for they shall be comforted.
Jesus was not preaching here on a social gospel for the poor and disenfranchised as so many commentators have tried to say. Our earlier chapter on 'conscience' spoke of the utter agony of soul that Luther, Bunyan and many others went through on their way into grace. This word for mourn could equally be translated 'wailing'. Luther 'wailed' in agony of conscience for years until he read Romans. John Bunyan wailed for 18 months, trying to find peace of mind. I 'got saved' every week for six months trying to find assurance. I love this Greek word for 'comfort', 'they shall be comforted', it's this wonderful word *parakaleó*, which means on this occasion to 'be brought very close and near'. The law kept you away, but grace brings you close and near.

Blessed are the meek, for they shall inherit the earth.
It's not weak but meek, sometimes translated 'humility'. But meekness has a stronger meaning; literally, it means 'harnessed strength'. And look at what's promised in Scripture: the whole earth. Isn't that what God promised Abraham?

Clearly, God's promise to give the whole earth
to Abraham and his descendants was based not
on his obedience to God's law, but on a right
relationship with God that comes by faith.

(ROMANS 4:13, NLT)

There it is. It cannot be clearer. This promise of whole earth inheritance was not based on obedience to God's law, but on faith and a right relationship with God. We've now stepped right on into Abraham's legacy. The big question is, will we let God harness us to the gospel of grace, or will we still press on, hitched to the wrong wagon of law and effort? It takes meekness to walk in grace.

Blessed are those who hunger and thirst for righteousness,
for they shall be filled.

We know already that a law-living life can never bring us to the place of satisfaction. The law is designed to always leave you unsatisfied. It's always, *I must try harder; I must do better.* Enough will never be enough.

However, if we realise that this kind of righteousness is an imputed gift, given by grace and received by faith, then it's the knowledge, understanding and revelation of this and all that it is, all that it offers, and all that it contains that we hunger for. Then we will be filled and satisfied, and this Greek word for satisfied means 'gorged'; or 'abundance'. Paul was confirming the same when he wrote Romans 5:17:

For if, by the trespass of the one man, death reigned through that one man, how much more will those who receive God's abundant provision of grace and of the gift of righteousness reign in life through the one man, Jesus Christ!

(ROMANS 5:17, NIV)

Life with grace is always a 'much more' life. Just like the Ten Commandments had two halves, one vertical (Godward) and the other horizontal (manward), so Jesus' teaching follows that pattern. Vertical kingdom connection affects horizontally lived life.

Blessed are the merciful, for they shall obtain mercy.
Strong's Greek dictionary defines mercy as *compassionate in word or deed especially by divine grace.* [22] Where would we be if we did not receive God's mercy daily? We could well agree with Phillip Henry who said, *If the end of one mercy were not the beginning of another, we would be undone.* [23] In other words, this kind of compassion or mercy is not simply human, it's accepting God's mercy to us and then allowing it to flow through us to others. Not only are grace-filled people generous, they are merciful.

I have noted and often seen that God's mercy or compassion when acted through me often tends to bring in the supernatural, just as it did with Jesus. Both the healing miracles and the supernatural supplies, like feeding the five thousand, were instigated by God's manifest compassion or mercy felt and freed in the life of Jesus. We often read the phrase *"And Jesus, moved with compassion . . ."* preceding a miracle.

One time a dear friend turned up at my door deeply concerned and downcast. Peter Pretorius, with his wife, Ann, started a most amazing work called Joint Aid Management (JAM). JAM, now led by their son Isak, is an incredible humanitarian aid and development organization that feeds over a million kids a year across Africa, as well as a host of other aid initiatives.

This was around 2010 and one of the world's worst recessions had hit the planet. Peter told me that as a consequence, he had just lost £1.5 million of funding from a particular source who now could no longer keep his promise, with the knock-on effect immediately cutting food supply to 120,000 kids. They needed the money there and then, not at the end of a six-month grant application, or else these kids would die. I so wanted to help but did not have that kind of money. In fact, we were under intense pressure ourselves.

As we talked over dinner, it came to my mind that a businessman I knew, who lived a few hours away, might help. His generous trust fund often did help so many projects, but had never given like that to JAM. Then there was a strict due process — due diligence, formalities, applications, supporting documents, etc. — that had to be submitted to their board, which only sat at certain times. Furthermore, this businessman travelled the world, and like so many, extremely busy. Still, I made a call only to find that this man was at home, and he kindly invited us up the next day. Within 24 hours we had a cheque for £1.5 million and 120,000 children's lives were saved.

I hadn't seen something like that happen before. But I have seen astonishing supplies of buildings, food, money and much more as God moves in mercy by releasing mercy to the merciful.

In the same year, we supernaturally bought a large bank's headquarters for our main base and Bible college. We bought it for several million pounds. When I agreed to the purchase, I didn't have one pound. God supernaturally supplied from the most unusual sources in a total miraculous way. We call it our miracle building. We had been shown mercy, albeit by God's gracious supply, and we in turn were shown mercy also by God's gracious supply. I love this life with God. This life is way beyond law-living, it's God being God with ready recipients.

Blessed are the pure in heart, for they shall see God.
Recently, my wife has taken up a new hobby, treasure hunting with metal detectors. It's often a lot of fun and excitement as we hear the 'dings' of the machine mark out a target. We live in an old property, steeped in history, so we have made some good ancient finds. But we have also found a ton of buried junk. As we got to know the gadget, we learned how to tune out iron trash and only look for the good stuff. But that isn't so easy when the metal is an alloy. Mixed metals sound like precious metals and may prove to be a wasted dig.

This phrase 'pure in heart' means 'pure, clear, unmixed or unalloyed'. [24] The challenge we have in our spiritual journey is that we can believe in a hybrid gospel, an alloy, a mixture of law and grace. This is often more deadly than law on its own. But if we stay, standing unmovable on God's grace and Christ's work, we will see God. We will see God manifest in power, come through in salvation, stir up in healings and demonstrate mighty signs and wonders. I have seen so many of these things happen right here in our community.

Regrettably, in my view, we have seen too many books written on 'works based ministry leading to power in life or service'. Consequently, thousands of people have prayed more, fasted more, given more or tried more . . . to only end up getting no more. All of these practices are good and right, but not right when you make them the pathway to seeing God move. There is only one pathway, the pure gospel of grace, unmixed and unalloyed. The clearer that is, the bigger the breakthroughs.

Blessed are the peacemakers, for they shall be called sons of God. Peace making is very different to peace keeping. I have a friend who is a major in the British Army. He was posted to Bosnia by the UN (United Nations) as a peacekeeper during the terrible troubles that happened there. He told me it was the worst posting of his career. Peacekeepers are ordered by the UN to never engage, not draw their weapons and never get involved. They were there simply to keep two warring factions apart. He watched terrible atrocities take place right in front of his own eyes but couldn't do a thing about it. The perpetrators knew the limitations of the UN forces and capitalised on it at every turn.

The world is in turmoil, and we have the solution. There is one command that does come from heaven — *engage*. We cannot stand back and do nothing. Just because we cannot change everything in our world does not mean we can't change something.

Predominantly, we are to preach the gospel and enable men and women to make their peace with God.

The thing I hate the most about the law-living mindset is that it nearly always freezes people for effective action. There is such concern on getting sin-free and right with God, with the added burden of guilt and condemnation, that the rest of the world goes to hell and we don't even notice. How many of God's people have their hands tied behind their backs because they don't feel worthy, or don't feel ready to engage?

Peace making is also an ongoing attitude. To be a peacemaker means to be one who bands people together. Grace pulls people together not drive them apart. The puritan Richard Baxter said, *'He that is not a son of peace is not a son of God'.* [25] In the same era, Thomas Brooks preached that we may labour mightily for a healing spirit. We have a guiding mantra around our churches, 'Find a need and meet it; find a hurt and heal it'.

Blessed are they who are persecuted for righteousness' sake, for theirs is the kingdom of heaven.
Jesus ends this part of His discourse with a warning that this kind of life He had just outlined will not go unchallenged, particularly by the religious classes.

Persecution comes in different ways. We have had pastors killed in India for just being Christian. Our children at the orphanage there have on multiple occasions been harassed because they are Christian. The global persecution of Christians is on a disturbing growing trend. A Chinese pastor once gave me his calling card, and his mantra, written on the back was *faithful unto death.*

You can be persecuted for just being different, especially in our woke world. A law is being created in my country known as the 'hate crime bill', and unless God intervenes, it will be passed. In concept, it sounds great, but in essence, it's going to be a huge challenge for Christians or others of other faiths for that matter, in that expressing a biblical opinion on sexuality, marriage or identity will potentially be a crime. But there is an expression which says: *Faith makes things possible, not easy.*

Benjamin Fernando said, *'Persecution is one of the surest signs of the genuineness of our Christianity'*. [26] Preaching a grace-filled gospel will get you into deep trouble with many other Christians, never mind the world out there. Religious people hate a grace-filled message even more than they love their legalistic ways.

The Pharisees were raging against Paul and wanted him killed for preaching this outrageous gospel that righteousness by faith in Christ alone was available to any and all. They stirred up the crowd who went on to stone him outside the city wall of Lystra. Some say in reading this account, placed alongside other readings, that Paul did actually die, and it was the disciples who circled around him that raised him from the dead.

In any event, it was the most awful of experiences. Yet when he did get back up on his feet, do you know what he did? He walked straight back into the same city. He left Lystra the next day to preach in Derbe, but later returned to Lystra to teach and preach again. How do you stop a person like that?

Jesus was doing more than vision casting in His Sermon on the Mount. He was laying out both a hope and a call to a cause. Paul had something bigger than a vision, he had a cause. You might live for a vision, but you will be willing to die for a cause. Jesus also said on more than one occasion, *"For this cause came I . . ."* (John 12:27, KJV).

We are actually promised the kingdom of God. We read:

> *"Do not be afraid, little flock, for your Father*
> *has been pleased to give you the kingdom."*
> **(LUKE 12:32, NIV)**

The 'little flock' were a handful of followers who after the cross, resurrection and Pentecost, went on in one generation to reach most of the known world. The kingdom of God is bigger than you or me, bigger than the church even, and destined, just like Daniel prophesied, to never fail or be handed over to another.

> *"But the saints of the Highest One will receive the kingdom*
> *and possess the kingdom forever, for all ages to come."*
> **(DANIEL 7:18, NASB 1995)**

If your biggest hope is heaven when you die, then your hope is far too small. There will be a resurrection around here one day, a new heaven and a new earth, and the whole kingdom of God will come into its eternal climax. The only kingdom that will prevail in this world is not of this world.

When it comes to morality and behaviour, if the law could have, it would have. It would have produced the right fruit in the soul and life of an individual, and in so doing, would have negated the need for Jesus ever to come. But the law could only produce bare trees and barren fields. However, Jesus did come. At one moment He said, *"It is finished,"* but in truth, it was as if it had only just begun.

'Everyone wants the kingdom of God, but few want it first'.

CHARLES L. VENABLE

8

Promises, Promises

*'The promises of God have never borrowed
help from moral probabilities'.*
THOMAS SHERLOCK

Forty years ago, Sue and I married on Valentine's Day. It was
a beautiful day with the bluest of skies. On that day we gave
ourselves one to the other. There were all kinds of people
present — family, friends, the minister — and God was present
too. They were all witnesses to our marriage and joyfully
celebrated with us.

What exactly did we do on that day? How do people give
themselves one to another in a life-long union that brings
two very different individuals together? What really makes
a marriage, at least in the eyes of the law? Actually, the marriage contract is quite a simple idea; we, like many others, gave

ourselves one to the other by making promises, and our guests were witnesses to that fact. We call these promises vows, our wedding vows. And we made vows that went something like: 'For better, for worse; for richer, for poorer; in sickness and in health; until death do us part'.

Marriage is a relationship built on promises, and for the last 40 years, every day of our lives, by the grace of God, that's what we've been trying to do. Keep promises. We have a marriage certificate, although I cannot remember the last time I looked at it. I know where to find it, but I don't go into the drawer every day to check to see if we're still married. The substance of our marriage isn't the certificate, it's the promises we made, ones which we take very seriously. We made those promises because we wanted to, not because we were forced to.

One time, Sue and I were walking down a street in Eastern India, having just visited our orphanage. We stopped to chat with a family who spoke English, and they kindly invited us into their home. The husband was a retired Army major, and he had two beautiful daughters in their late teens. The girls sat on the floor and starred at us, having never been this close to white people before. Then one of the girls boldly asked, 'Was yours a love marriage?' We had never been asked such a question before — that was a first. We realised that this was her dream and a much-discussed topic of conversation in their house, as an arranged marriage with a complete stranger was about to be her fate. 'Yes', we said. 'Ours was a love marriage'.

Ours was a love marriage; we were not coerced or forced into it. However, we think God was behind it, so you could say that it was arranged.

God, in the same way, commits Himself into relationships. He didn't have to, He was not coerced into it, He wanted to! This relationship between God and us is a love relationship established and only made possible by grace. Having initiated the relationship, just like in a marriage, this God relationship works on promises. God gives Himself by making promises, and when He does, it's called a covenant. If we, being human, take our promises very seriously, how much more does God?

This is the New Covenant, which Jesus established with His own precious blood, He said:

> "... for this is my blood, which confirms the
> covenant between God and his people. It is poured
> out as a sacrifice to forgive the sins of many."
> (MATTHEW 26:28, NLT)

The Remarkable Relationship

In our world, only humans can marry. In all marriages everywhere, only one human can marry another.

So how can we fallen human beings enter into a relationship with God, who is altogether different to us? How do we get into the 'God-class' to participate in a relationship with Him? Either

He has to become like one of us, or we have to become like Him. Remarkably, BOTH things happened.

There is some truth in Joan Osborne's song 'One of Us'. She asks the question, 'What if God was one of us?'

If God had a name what would it be?
And would you call it to his face?
If you were faced with Him in all His glory
What would you ask if you had just one question?

God became man, and His name is Jesus. He had a face, a body and a very real presence. Guessing about what God looked like came to an end as soon as Jesus arrived.

It's remarkable that God should become human, but how does a human become like God?

There are only two ways that this could happen. You can try to enter the God-class of being by becoming as perfect and as holy as He is. You couldn't ever become God of course, as there is only one Almighty, but partaking of divine nature is another matter. And so that we are clear and understand what that means, He gave us the Law. Can we keep it? Not a chance, no one can.

So, the only other option is for God, by grace, to do something that we could not do for ourselves: He would have to change us, remake us to be as He is.

The first thing that grace does when it impacts your life is to make you like God — not the last thing. Many Christians are of the opinion that it's the last thing God does. In fact, they think you don't become like God until the day you die and go to heaven. The truth is, it's the first thing that God does, so that you can walk with Him and enjoy this amazing relationship. We are elevated into the God-class of being. How is this possible? We read:

> And because of his glory and excellence, he has given
> us great and precious promises. These are the promises
> that enable you to share his divine nature and escape
> the world's corruption caused by human desires.
>
> **(2 PETER 1:4, NLT)**

Here we are back at promises again. God gives us promises, and in so doing gives us Himself.

I see these promises as being in two very distinct and important categories. Promises that get you INTO His family and promises that enable you to enjoy the benefits of being a part of that family.

From the moment Adam and Eve fell, God promised recovery. We read of it in Genesis 3:15, a clear declaration that Jesus would one day come and destroy the devil's work. God kept that promise.

God promised Abraham that through his descendants all the families of the earth would be blessed. Jesus, born as a Jew, as a son of Abraham, brought a new dawn for all. God kept that promise.

God promised through Isaiah that a smitten saviour would die for our sins, diseases and transgressions. God kept that promise.

God promised Ezekiel that He would put a new heart and a new spirit inside His people. God has kept that promise; we can now be born again.

God promised the prophet Joel that He would send the Holy Spirit to live in men and women, sons and daughters. God kept that promise.

As far as these promises, and so many like them, are concerned, all we have to do is receive them. It's as easy as that; it really is as good as that. Astronomical grace!

Conditions or Applications?

Since we insist on building our world on hard work and self-effort, we so quickly focus on our side of the bargain. It takes two to make a marriage, so it must take the two of us, (God and us) to make this relationship work, isn't that right? Surely, we must have to do something?

The only thing that you have to do is believe and receive. That's why it's grace. Until you are IN God's family, you will never have any ability to keep your side of the contract. That's why Peter wrote that by and through these precious promises we escape the corruption or sin in this world. We add nothing to our own salvation — it's all God.

God, having brought us into this family, then gives Himself in that relationship unreservedly. God doesn't stand back at a distance and watch us over the horizon. He gives Himself into that relationship passionately, intimately, affectionately, gladly, and generously. He lavishes His heart and all that He has on us.

God gives himself to you and to me through His promises. In the same way that Sue and I made promises one to another, God gives Himself to you through His promises. He makes promises. And when He makes those promises, that is the way in which God takes of what He is, and what He has, and says, *It's yours.*

Now to be clear, God is a free agent. No one can bend his arm up behind his back to make Him do what He doesn't want to do. He didn't have to make any promise at all. So, He chose to make promises. The thing is, once He made the promises, He's bound by them. It was Hudson Taylor who said, *'There is a living God. He has spoken in the Bible. He means what he says and will do all He has promised'.* [27]

I don't know how many promises there are, I haven't actually counted them. Some tell me there is a promise for every situation. Whatever circumstance you're in today, perhaps a debt problem, maybe you need a job, or you're facing a sickness? There could be a relationship problem in your family. Maybe your kids aren't talking to you. Perhaps you're anxious and very, very worried about certain things. There is a promise for that situation and every situation. Promises like:

- *"Never will I leave you; never will I forsake you."* (Hebrews 13:5, NIV)

- *"For where two or three are gathered together in My name, I am there in the midst of them."* (Matthew 18:20, NKJV)

- *"By His stripes we are healed."* (Isaiah 53:5, NKJV)

- *"My grace is sufficient for you."* (2 Corinthians 12:9, NIV)

- *"I came that they may have and enjoy life, and have it in abundance."* (John 10:10, AMP)

- *"My God will supply all your needs according to His riches in Christ Jesus."* (Philippians 4:19, NASB)

- *"Every place that the sole of your foot will tread upon I have given you, as I said to Moses."* (Joshua 1:3, NKJV)

We could go on and on and on; there is a promise for every situation. Someone told me there's a promise for every day of the year. Another person said that there are more than 3,000 promises in God's Word. God has given Himself to you through His promise. When God gives Himself to you in a promise, He means exactly what He said.

Over the centuries, great men and women have discovered that the key to receiving astronomical grace is none other than standing on God's promises.

- Matthew Henry: *'God never promises more than he can perform'.* [28]

- William Carey: *'My future is as bright as the promises of God'.* [29]

- F.B. Meyer: *'We must learn to put down our foot upon the Promises of God's Word, and say: "These are mine by right, and shall be mine in actual enjoyment"'.* [30]

- C.H. Spurgeon: *'God never out-promised Himself yet'.* [31]

- Again, Spurgeon: *'If you appropriate a promise it will not be pilfering: you may take it boldly and say, "This is mine"'.* [32]

- Geoffrey Wilson said, *'Christ is the fulfiller and fulfilment of all the promises of God, because He's the sum and substance of them'.* [33]

In his day, Spurgeon packed out his church week in, week out. Every Monday, the national newspapers reported on what he said on Sunday. He sold more than 32 million publications of his messages in 17 languages. He prospered exceedingly. How did you do that, Mr Spurgeon? His reply would be, *'If you appropriate a promise it will not be pilfering, you may take it boldly and say this is mine'*. He also said, 'The Lord does not play at promising'.

The most important thing about your life today is the promise you're carrying. What's the promise on your mind, in your heart right now? This is how God gives Himself to you. In 1 Corinthians 3, Paul writes to the church and asks them why they are living like mere men. We might say that we are just that — ordinary people. But when we become a part of God's family and astronomical grace is flowing towards you, we above all should be living at a whole different plane.

How do we get onto that plane? God gives Himself by His promises. Nearly all Christians will believe what I've just been saying. They believe that God is good, God keeps his word, God has made promises, there is a promise for every situation, and there is a promise for every day — they believe it. But they don't experience it. It's not even in their expectation. You know why? They have either consciously or subconsciously disengaged for the following reason.

They go on to read the promises and find that nearly all of those promises have conditions.

We look into the Word, and we see the promises and we find conditions attached. You know God gives the promise, but once you hear of a condition, you switch from one foot to the other. Instead of leaning on God, you start leaning on your ability to keep the condition. And in the back of our minds and all too often in the depths of our heart, we either hear a voice saying, *But you didn't keep the condition* or *You only sometimes keep the condition* or *You must try harder to keep that condition.* So, where has our focus gone? It's gone from looking to God who gives the promise, to our ability to keep the condition.

Now, I've got good news for you today, no matter what the promise is, you already qualify.

Here's a key verse:

> *For as many as the promises of God are,*
> (see Paul didn't count the promises either)
> *in Him they are yes; therefore through Him also*
> *is our Amen to the glory of God through us.*
> (2 CORINTHIANS 1:20, NASB)

Another translation:

> *For all of God's promises have been fulfilled in Christ with*
> *a resounding "Yes!" And through Christ, our "Amen"*
> *(which means "Yes") ascends to God for his glory.*
> (2 CORINTHIANS 1:20, NLT)

I want to tell you, the revelation I got when preparing this message has completely transformed and changed my life. You qualify because HE qualifies. Jesus is the only one who ever met and fully complied with every condition attached to the promises.

Paul reminds us in Ephesians that we should honour our mothers and our fathers, for this is the first commandment with a promise — we will live long on the earth. We all want to live long, but who amongst us has honoured our parents at all times, on each and every occasion without fault or failure? We dishonour once — we forfeit the promise. But when I'm standing in my new location, my new position in Christ, He qualifies, so I qualify. It's simply left to me to say, 'Amen', or, 'I agree, so be it'. It's not that I don't honour my parents, it's that my confidence in the promise is not in my ability to keep the conditions, but in God's ability to fulfil it to me because of Christ and astronomical grace. This is a game changer!

There is a very famous promise passage of the Bible, Deuteronomy 30:19. In this chapter we read *"I have set before you life and death, blessings and curses. Now choose life, so that you and your children may live"* (NIV). It's a message to Israel as they prepare to move on and into the promised land, or the **land of promise**. He has already made some huge promises:

If you fully obey the L*ord* *your God and carefully*
follow all his commands I give you today, the L*ord*
your God will set you high above all the nations
on earth. All these blessings will come on you and
accompany you if you obey the L*ord* *your God:*
You will be blessed in the city and blessed in the country.
The fruit of your womb will be blessed, and the crops
of your land and the young of your livestock — the
calves of your herds and the lambs of your flocks.
Your basket and your kneading trough will be blessed.
You will be blessed when you come in
and blessed when you go out.

(DEUTERONOMY 28:1-6, NIV)

These and many more blessings are listed, so much so that the conclusion is that all nations will call Israel blessed. The challenge lies in the conditions attached to all of these promises. The chapter opens by saying:

> *If you fully obey the* Lord *your God and carefully follow*
> *all his commands I give you today, the* Lord *your God*
> *will set you high above all the nations on earth.*
> (DEUTERONOMY 28:1, NIV)

To make matters worse, a failure to keep these laws will result in cursing. We read:

> *However, if you do not obey the* Lord *your God*
> *and do not carefully follow all his commands*
> *and decrees I am giving you today, all these*
> *curses will come on you and overtake you.*
> (DEUTERONOMY 28:15, NIV)

Left at first read, we are all in big trouble, just as they were then. They did not keep the commandments and were very soon carried off into exile, cursed. But there is a New Testament after the Old, and in that we're told that not only did Jesus keep every part of every condition, but He also became a curse for you and me.

> *Christ redeemed us from the curse of the Law,*
> *having become a curse for us — for it is written:*
> "CURSED IS EVERYONE WHO HANGS ON A TREE."
> (GALATIANS 3:13, NASB)

That cross was a cursed cross, but for us, it's the greatest blessing ever. It's there that the divine exchange took place.

Jesus became the worst of men as every sin was placed on Him, that we might be the best of men, as all that was His was laid to our account.

When I read the Old Testament, I find God connecting with people on the basis of conditions. Why? As yet Jesus hadn't come, there hadn't been a final and full blood sacrifice, God hadn't yet given His only Son, there had been no cross, there had been no permanent solution for the sins of mankind. That was yet to come. So, the best they could do was try their hardest to keep the law. And when they didn't and failed, they had to get so many bulls and so many goats and so many animals to cover every single failure, they were never away from sacrifices.

We should not read Old Testament promises, prayers or practices as if the cross never happened or Jesus never came. We are not standing where they once stood. Everything has changed.

What if we could have kept the condition of every promise? In that split second, we would say, *Look at what I did.* In that split second, our own self-righteousness would already be separating us from God, it would be separating us from grace

So, what about these promises then? Do they just hang in the air? No, 2,000 years ago, a Man came to this earth and walked this planet, keeping every condition, every rule, every precept, He kept every point. Even when He defended His disciples for picking grain on the Sabbath day and breaking the fourth commandment, He Himself was not. He kept the law in every point.

And when He died in our place, all of our failures were placed on Him, while all of His rightness was placed on us. Paul says, *I don't know how many promises there are, but every one of them is yes in Christ Jesus. In Him we qualify*. In other words, there may be a condition, but it's already met because the condition is Christ. And the last quote from the faith quotes above said:

'Christ is the fulfiller and fulfilment of all the promises of God because He is the sum and substance of them'. [34]

GEOFFREY WILSON

God gave Himself to us in promises, and when you get a hold of that promise, it doesn't at all depend upon you for its fulfilment. Now, I know some of you believe it does. That's why you're not experiencing the promise. Once you settle in your heart that it doesn't depend upon you, but upon Him — the breakthroughs come. This is astronomical grace. I know I'm undeserving, I know I missed the mark, I know at best I only keep the conditions sometimes, but in Him, I say, So let it be, every one of them are yes.

C.H. Spurgeon said these profound words:

'The immutable word of promise is and ever must be the pure rule of God's giving. Consider a little, while I make a further observation, namely that against this no other rule can stand. With a rule of God's promise no other law, supposed or real, can ever come into conflict. You see, the law of deserving is sometimes set up against this rule. But it cannot prevail. Says one, I cannot think that God can or will save me, for there is no good thing in me, you speak rightly, there isn't anything good in you and

your fear cannot be removed if God is to act towards you upon the rule of deserving. But if you believe on his son Jesus, that rule of deserving will not operate. The Lord will act towards you, according to the rule of his promise. For the promise never was, and is not, founded upon your merits. It was freely made and it would be as freely kept. If you inquire how your ill disseverance can be met, let me remind you of Jesus, who came to save you from your sins. The boundless deserving's of the Lord Jesus are set to your account and your terrible demerits, they're neutralized once and for all. The law of merit would sentence you to distraction, as you stand in your own proper person. But he that believes is not under the law, but under grace. And when under grace, the great Lord deals with men, according to pure mercy as revealed in his promise. You do not stagger or need to start at the promise through unbelief, but reckon that he who has promised is also able to perform. Don't limit the holy one of Israel by dreaming that his love is limited by your capacity. The volume of the river is not computed by the dryness of the desert through which it flows, there is no logical proportion between the two. Even with half an eye, one can see that there is no calculating the extent of infinite love by measuring it against human weakness. The operations of almighty grace are not limited by mortal strength, nor by my want of strength. God's power is the thing that will keep God's promises. It's not your weakness that can defeat God's Promise, nor your strength that can fulfil it. For he that spoke the word will himself make it good. It is neither your business, or mine to try and keep God's promise; that is his office and not ours. Poor helpless one, why don't you attach your heavy wagon of incapacity to the engine of the promise, and you will be drawn along the lines of duty and blessing and see God do so much more, though you are dead you will live. Though you have weakness you shall be strong. This shall not affect the certainty of the divine engagement, for the power of the promise lies in him who made the promise'. [35]

Practise the Promise

I know what you're thinking. *Does that mean I don't have to do anything as far as any of these amazing promises are concerned?* I went back to God with the same question. I remember telling the Lord, *'When I read many of your promises, Lord, those comments sure sound like conditions to be fulfilled on my part!'*

When I read some of those promises, such as, *"Bring the whole tithe into the storehouse, so that there may be food in My house, and put Me to the test now in this,"* says the LORD *of armies, "if I do not open for you the windows of heaven and pour out for you a blessing until it overflows"* (Malachi 3:10, NASB). It sure sounds like a condition to me.

Are those conditions taken away by what I'm reading post-Christ, post-cross and now we have the New Testament? So, the

Holy Spirit whispered into my heart, *'People refer to them as conditions; they're no longer conditions, they're applications'.*

You see, I may drive a powerful car and the manufacturer's handbook might say that this car will do 140 miles an hour. So, I may be out visiting our German churches and I might be sitting on the no speed restriction Autobahn. I might say I really, truly believe that this car will do 140 miles an hour. But simply believing it won't make it so, and definitely won't make it go and get up to that speed. Is the manufacturer wrong? No. Is the car capable of doing 140 miles an hour. Yes! Does it depend upon me pushing it? No, the power is in the engine. What do I have to do? Well, you sit in the car, start the engine, you engage the gear, and you press that accelerator. You get on the Autobahn and you're away. The manufacturer speaks the truth; it can do it, and now I'm up to that speed. I'm going flat out, this thing does exactly what it said it could do.

We read these important verses:

> *But someone may well say, "You have faith and I have works; show me your faith without the works, and I will show you my faith by my works." . . . For just as the body without the spirit is dead, so also faith without works is dead.*
> (JAMES 2:18, 26, NASB)

When it comes to the promises of God, we must have faith in the God of the promise.

When I apply my faith by stepping up and out, and then into the biblical application, James sees that as 'works of faith'. It has nothing to do with your salvation or your standing in Christ; it's not that kind of a work. It's an act of faith in the promise, the God of the promise and that all conditions are met in Christ — so here goes!

It looks like this: We read, *"I am the* LORD, *who heals you"* (Exodus 15:26, NIV). Does God keep his word? Are you convinced? Is He a man that he should lie or change his mind? Is Jesus Christ the same yesterday, today and forever? Will He heal now? Of course He will. Then, how do I apply the promise? Sitting there saying it is not going to get you well, and asking yourself if you deserve it will definitely end up negatively, so standing in all that Christ has done, how do I proceed?

There are at least two applications in the Bible concerning this point. Either will work. We are told to lay hands on the sick and they will recover, or if you are already a Christian and a part of a church, then such members should call for the elders, the overseers of the church, who must come and anoint you with oil. The prayer of faith will heal the sick and even if you have sinned, you will be forgiven.

So, is it a condition? No, it's an application. It shows me how to put that promise into action. Well, what about finances? The Word says, *"And my God shall supply all your need according to His riches in glory by Christ Jesus"* (Philippians 4:19, NKJV). We are called believers. Such a person is someone who relies and acts upon what he hears. You see the promise is true, but to process promise, we must also apply its truth.

So, when the Bible says, *"Bring the whole tithe into the store-house, so that there may be food in My house, and put Me to the test now in this," says the* LORD *of armies, "if I do not open for you the windows of heaven and pour out for you a blessing until it overflows"* (Malachi 3:10, NASB). God is the giver of the promise, the application is what unlocks it in my life. If I don't apply it, the promise stands unfulfilled. When I apply it, it's a demonstration of my faith. So, when things are challenging financially in my life and God still says put Him first, and I trust him by applying it, the promise is fulfilled. It's nothing to do with me. I've turned on the engine, I've put it into gear, now God provides the power.

On the subject of tithing, I have read grace teachers say it's now an obsolete, unnecessary practice. That's quite a mistake in my mind. Tithing started with the biggest faith person of all, Abraham. He is held up for us as the father of all who believe. All of this happened **before** the Law ever came. So tithing was nothing to do with a legalistic practice. Further, on this subject or any other issue, such teachers fail to understand the principles of continuity or discontinuity.

In other words, what carries over into the New Testament life from the old? Many things discontinue because they find their real fulfilment in Christ. They were the shadow, He is the substance. So, we don't continue with sacrifices, Jesus was the final Lamb of God who takes away the sins of the world. We don't continue with circumcision, in that water baptism has now taken its place according to Peter. We don't even continue with Sabbath keeping, since Christ is our Sabbath according to Paul. In each and every place where something is discontinued, we are told so in the New Testament, and we are told why. But no such mention is ever said or made of tithing. In fact, we are encouraged by way of example in Hebrews to keep going on the matter of tithing.

Go Large

When God enters my human existence, and steps into my world, He tries to get me to understand how big He is, how huge His grace is and just how far it will take me.

We think that finding Christ is just like getting a passport into a new country — the kingdom of God. We are in, and over the border, but the King of this Kingdom lives in some palace or castle far away. We are glad that we are in though, right? But not only are we in — we are IN!

Out of his fullness we have all received
grace in place of grace already given.
(JOHN 1:16, NIV)

This grace takes us as far as it's possible to go. It's contrary to everything we have ever learned. Jesus did this with the disciples all the time. He tried to get them to understand the magnitude of this life.

Jesus goes to a wedding with His disciples to find that they've ran out of wine, AFTER they had already drunk plenty. He's asked to help by His mother, Mary, and so we have the first miracle. Most pastors at that wedding would say, *"Don't you boys think you've had enough?"* But Jesus created six jars of brand new, yet vintage quality, wine. There were 20–30 gallons of water in each jar, usually kept for ritual, religious ceremonial cleansing. That's 120–180 gallons of wine, 680 litres, or just over 900 bottles of vintage wine. Moses' first miracle turned water into blood; Jesus' first miracle turned water into wine. The law always brings judgment, but grace always brings life — and lots of it.

On another occasion, the disciples had been fishing all night and caught nothing. 'Put your net down on the righthand side', Jesus yells. They caught so many fish that the catch nearly sank two boats.

There was once a conference on the hillside with some 10,000 people, with 5,000 men alone. The people got hungry, and there was no food. 'You feed them', Jesus says. With what? They receive an offering from a little boy of five loaves and two fish. Jesus blesses it, breaks it and everyone has more than enough. They even pick up 12 baskets of leftovers. Jesus was trying to get them to have a large, generous, astronomical-grace, multitude mindset.

I had a good friend who owned a large business with several subsidiaries. He decided it was time to sell up and move on. He hired top business consultants in London to handle the sale of his company. They met with him and his directors and told them that they should first prepare a one, three and five year business plan, showing and demonstrating the potential of the business. They dutifully complied, or so they thought.

When they reported back to these consultants with their business plans, they were stopped short in their presentation by the comment, *'What have you done? We did not intend for you to make those plans with your current and present resources, but we wanted you to imagine that a large global player had bought you out. What could be done with their vast resources?'*

They had to go back to the drawing board and rethink. In the final sale, they achieved eight times more for the sale than expected, since a global player did buy them out and went on to invest heavily. This amazing gospel is like that, we are invited to live life on all fronts from God's grace resources and they are truly astronomical.

'Christ, who is your righteousness before God, gives more value to your existence than you can imagine'. [36]

MARTIN LUTHER

9

The Exchanged Life

'The greatest of saints are the greatest receivers'. [37]

ALAN REDPATH

At one time in my life, I looked like I had a million dollars but was in reality, totally penniless. Consequently, I was not going to attract anyone's sympathy for the help I so desperately needed.

Sue and I had recently planted a new church which was doing well, but it needed a war chest, a cash flow injection, and so we proposed that we should take up a special offering amongst our congregation. Being leaders, we knew how important it was to go first in our giving and set the pace by example. We had taught our people that it wasn't equal giving, but it was equal sacrifice in moments like this. Each person had different and various amounts of disposable income, so we could not all give the same, but we could all step up to the plate and sacrifice the same.

A small amount to one family might be like that widow's mite we read of in Scripture, for they would be giving all they had, whilst to others, a large amount might be like small change. It was time to reach and a time to give.

Having set the vision and the date for this special offering, we set ourselves to pray and ask God as to what we as a couple should give ourselves. We decided that we would sell our almost new 'paid for' car and give the proceeds, and trust God for a new vehicle. The car sold, the giving day came, the offering was encouraging and so we set out to believe God for our new car.

Several frustrating months later, I was still without a car. I learned a great deal about faith in this moment, but the biggest lesson that I was about to learn was all about grace.

Having complained to God about my lack of transport, and pointed out the obedient step we took in selling the car and sowing the proceeds into that special offering, I then heard Him clearly ask me, *'Which car did you want?'* It seemed God had been waiting for me to get specific. I had just wanted any car, but God wanted more detail to answer this particular prayer.

So, then I got specific, from the brand down to the colour and even the interior colour combination. I chose a good, reliable brand and could see it already in my mind's eye but had no idea how it would ever land up in my driveway.

To cut a long story short, that very car was bought for me a few months later, and as I collected it from the dealership, the salesman told me how difficult that colour combination was to find. But my generous benefactor not only bought the car but more besides. He told me that I could not drive such a car dressed as I was. In those days we all wore suits and ties to preach, so he went and bought me a top-end Italian suit, with classy English shoes to match. I looked like a million bucks. The only challenge was I literally had no money; I was penniless.

The following day was Sunday, and I was booked to preach in a large church. I hardly had enough fuel to get there, and no money for fuel home.

Not daunted — I knew this church and they were always generous — I was confident that a suitable honorarium would be given before I left. In the event, after a great service, the pastor who was a close friend said, *'Sorry, Andrew, I'm in a rush today but will send you something in the post'*. Never doubting his word, I was now doubting my journey home.

I looked like I had everything but actually had nothing. Not one person looking on would ever be aware of my financial need. My lovely new car was parked outside, my suit and silk tie looked the prestigious part, but my pocket and bank account were empty. I continued to minister to people in the prayer line whilst being preoccupied with my own prayer and my own need in my own heart.

Then, out of the corner of my eye, I could see a poor elderly lady waiting to talk with me. I knew this lady since a few years earlier I had helped start this church and had led her to the Lord. I had been to her home and knew first-hand how poor she was. She had nothing, but lived mostly hand-to-mouth and on the kindness of others.

She reached out her hand to give me several folded bank notes. Telling me that God had told her that she was to go to church that day and give me all that she had. I found these words forming in my mouth, *I just can't accept this from you,* but even whilst the words were forming on my lips, I heard the Holy Spirit whisper in my heart: *Accept it or you will be walking home.*

I found it the hardest thing possible to receive from her that day. Everything inside me was contesting it. My pride, my embarrassment, my sense of self-sufficiency, even trying to find the sense of equity in the situation. Surely this wasn't right, couldn't be fair? This lady with next to nothing, and me with a fancy suit and a quality car? But the truth was I had nothing either.

Yet I knew that God in His grace had chosen this woman to meet my need in that moment. She was sowing this seed just like I had sown my car a few months earlier. I accepted the money, prayed that God would abundantly bless her in her sowing and made it home with a tank full of fuel.

I could hardly remember a time of feeling so humbled and yet so grateful. This story happened many years ago, but I remember it like it was today. I can still feel the emotion of receiving that money from her even as I write this story.

I lost all interest in that car from that point forwards, even though I had only just acquired it. Overnight it meant nothing to me. Don't get me wrong, I was so grateful for God who provided it and the man who gave it, but something else was going on in my heart.

Both this lady's action in giving and my reticence and difficulty in receiving turned over a thousand times in my mind. I realised that had the money come through a well-off person, I wouldn't have given it another thought, but the utter poverty, the obedience and the generosity of that lady as used by God that day was working something very deep within me.

Many cars have come and gone in my life since then, and we all now preach as far away from suits as possible, but the impact of that moment has always stayed with me. God did a bigger work of grace in my heart than the miracle of the answered prayer in my driveway. I learned about the power of active faith but realised all of it depended on the overwhelming grace of God.

Through prayer and faith, I received a car, but only the grace of God could keep me in it. And oftentimes, that grace comes through the most unlikely to the most undeserving, including me.

And that is, in reality, the true life of a believer.

People use their God-given faith to get saved but have yet to realise only the grace of God can keep them living that new life that they have now found.

The opening quote for this chapter from Alan Redpath continues as follows:

'The greatest of saints are the greatest of receivers. Let us believe that we receive, reckon on it, and live in the power of it, and so act on faith. All of the Lord Jesus Christ is mine at the moment of conversion, but I possess only as much of Him as by faith I claim'. [38]

Many of us look just like I did that Sunday when I received that beautiful offering. We look like we have it all together and no one looking on would know any different. Yet, so often underneath the façade of appearances and church learned behaviour, we wonder if we can make it through another day. Fears, phobias and anxieties, insecurities, bad habits, hidden sins and broken relationships lie buried beneath.

We know so well our utter powerlessness. It doesn't seem to change anything, but have we learned the power of an exchanged life? It is life made available by the grace of God.

We find it so hard to receive God's grace for ongoing forgiveness, permanent presence, unchangeable righteousness, unbroken promises and sheer undeserved blessings. Such is the magnitude of astronomical grace. We struggle to find the equity in the situation because the truth is we know that we just don't deserve it.

Yet we read and learn that Jesus gave all of Himself for all of us and never once took anything back. Jesus is our saviour, healer, sanctifier and high priest, He forgives, restores, empowers and equips. He truly is the Alpha and Omega of our lives, and as Redpath said, we need to possess all of Him, not just some of Him.

We again quote one of our key verses on this theme that underscores the need to be those receiving receivers:

> *For if by the transgression of the one, death reigned*
> *through the one, much more those who **receive** the*
> *abundance of grace and of the gift of righteousness*
> *will reign in life through the One, Jesus Christ*
> (ROMANS 5:17, NASB 1995)

It's not just receiving grace, but the abundance of grace.

Alan Redpath's quote comes from his study on the book of Joshua. As you may know, Joshua is told by God that he was being given the promised land in fulfilment of God's promise to Abraham, and that every place the sole of his foot would tread was his.

In other words, God's giving was for Joshua's taking. He still had to go and stand on it, and that was despite the walls, the giants, the iron chariots and the powerful kings that opposed him.

Likewise, grace has to be stood on! Grace has to be received; grace has to be accepted. We too have enemies to overcome. The enemies of guilt, shame and the condemnation that then follow. The devil who is called the 'accuser' is relentless and never gives up pointing out our flaws and faults along with the flaws of others we know and love. Then there are the enemies of religious expectation, such as perceived 'accepted or expected behaviour'.

It's no wonder that this word *'stand'* was one of the apostle Paul's most favourite words.

We've quoted it already, but here it is again:

Therefore, having been justified by faith, we have
peace with God through our Lord Jesus Christ,
through whom we also have obtained our introduction
*by faith into this grace in **which we stand; and***
we celebrate in hope of the glory of God.
(ROMANS 5:1–2, NASB)

There are three important things that we need to know if we are to truly maximise the life of grace and so find ourselves standing in it and standing on it.

A Clear Revelation

When we speak of revelation, we mean seeing something with the eye of your spirit, and once you have seen it, you cannot then unsee it. We call that a revelation.

The Old Testament book of Joshua has a corresponding New Testament book, which is the book of Ephesians. In Joshua, we read of a man leading a people to possess the promised land. Unlike some old-time hymns, the promised land is not symbolic of heaven, but a victorious life to be lived in the here and now. Joshua faced giants, battles and fortified Jericho. He made mistakes, prayed hard and fought through. Hardly a picture of heaven. None of these things will be needed there since no foes will be present.

In Ephesians, we are told of our position. We read, *"Blessed be the God and Father of our Lord Jesus Christ, who has blessed us with every spiritual blessing in the heavenly places in Christ"* (Ephesians 1:3, NASB). Again, this is not speaking of going to heaven, but teaches that as Jesus is sitting on a throne in these high-up heavenly places, we are positioned in Him here on earth.

The Christian does not work up towards victory, he works down from it! [39]

As you come to the last chapter of Joshua (chapter 24), you read of Joshua's parting words to the leaders and people of Israel. He summarises their journey starting with Abraham and concludes by challenging them with a choice and clear instruction.

But maybe the first thing that we should notice from this chapter is how many times God speaks in the divine first person. No less than 17 times in 12 verses, the divine personal pronoun is used.

In Joshua 24 (NASB) we read:

- *"I took your father Abraham"* (v. 3)

- *"I sent Moses and Aaron"* (v. 5)

- *"I brought your fathers out of Egypt"* (v. 6)

- *"Then I brought you to the land"* (v. 8)

- *"I handed them* (your enemies) *over to you"* (v. 11)

It is so easy for these people to forget that GOD DID IT. They are reminded that it wasn't their sword or their bow that won them the victory, but God.

This is the exact same principle taught by Paul in Ephesians:

But God, being rich in mercy, because of His great love
with which He loved us, even when we were dead in our
transgressions, made us alive together with Christ
(by grace you have been saved), and raised us up with
Him, and seated us with Him in the heavenly places in
Christ Jesus, so that in the ages to come He might show
the surpassing riches of His grace in kindness toward
us in Christ Jesus. For by grace you have been saved
through faith; and that not of yourselves, it is the gift of
God; not as a result of works, so that no one may boast.

(EPHESIANS 2:4–9, NASB 1995)

God saved you.

God filled you with the Holy Spirit.

God set you free.

It's God at the beginning, God in the middle and God at the end.

I often tell people that not only does God have Alpha Programmes (which is a hugely successful global outreach programme), but He has Omega Programmes. He will finish what He started within us.

Anything God wants out of us, God's grace will put into us.

And God's grace will keep us where God's will takes us.

Once that revelation is in our hearts, we will always want to live God-dependent and God-connected. This is what Jesus meant when He told us in John's gospel that He is the vine and we are the branches. He made it clear: *"apart from me you can do nothing"* (John 15:5, NIV).

The Divine Exchange

If you read Joshua chapter 24 (NIV), you might notice a very odd paradox. As Joshua sums up in his 'good-bye' speech, we read that he gives the Israelites a clear instruction and a very big challenge:

- *"Now fear the LORD and serve Him"* (v. 14)

- *"Choose for yourselves this day whom you will serve"* (v. 15)

Then the people answer,

- *"We too will serve the LORD, because He is our God"* (v. 18)

They give the correct response you would think, but surprisingly Joshua replies,

- *"You are not able to serve the LORD. He is a holy God"* (v. 19)

So, why did Joshua then ask the people to do something that he already knew couldn't be done, at least by them? The ask is clearly too big.

No doubt Joshua remembered well the sad events at Mount Sinai when the law was given. The people very confidently replied then that they would and could keep all God requested. But even in that first day, 3,000 died because they failed to keep even the first commandment and were found to be worshipping a golden calf.

The truth is that the life we are to live must be a divine exchanged life.

I can't but *HE* can.

Paul understood this when he wrote:

> *I am crucified with Christ: nevertheless I live; yet*
> *not I, but Christ liveth in me: and the life which I*
> *now live in the flesh I live by the faith of the Son of*
> *God, who loved me, and gave himself for me.*
>
> **(GALATIANS 2:20, KJV)**

The key to a maximised grace-filled life is actually a fully surrendered life. I have to lose my life to find it. I have to give in to win.

That great missionary to China, Hudson Taylor, tells of his greatest key to breakthrough:

'*It's not what Hudson Taylor does for God that matters, but what God does through Hudson Taylor*'. [40]

This concept is often repeated throughout the Scriptures. One such example is in the book of Jeremiah:

> *Thus says the* LORD, *"Cursed is the man who*
> *trusts in mankind and makes flesh his strength,*
> *and whose heart turns away from the* LORD.
>
> **(JEREMIAH 17:5, NASB 1995)**

We cannot trust in our own ability for one moment. But we should trust in God's grace forever.

As a new Christian, I had a very difficult experience. A certain man who had become a spiritual father to me died suddenly. I was devastated and confused. Not having long been in the faith and still being just a teenager, I was angry at God. How could He do, or at least allow such a thing? I felt this particularly hard in that my own father had left us when I was just a toddler, and so this man really had become a father figure in my life.

On hearing the news of his death, I went home and decided that I would give up on God. I threw my Bible into the corner of my bedroom and with a heart full of intent said, *That's it. I will never pick that book up again.*

Then the strangest thing happened.

In the middle of the night, I woke up to a vision. This vision was like a movie being played out on the wall of my bedroom. As I looked on, a Bible verse was being typed out underneath it. Not being familiar with the Bible, I didn't know it, but as it wrote, the text came up with it. It read:

> *But they that wait upon the* LORD *shall renew their strength;*
> *they shall mount up with wings as eagles; they shall run,*
> *and not be weary; and they shall walk, and not faint.*
>
> **(ISAIAH 40:31, KJV)**

I scrambled to find the Bible I had thrown into the corner and picked it up to find this verse.

The verse speaks of *the exchanged life.* Swopping out my weakness for His strength, my ignorance for His wisdom, my inability for His supernatural ability. Whilst that experience did not remove the loss I felt in my heart, it placed within me an absolute certainty that God was with me and He would not be leaving, not now, not ever.

I have since learned that I can't even love my own wife or family properly unless I apply the exchanged life principle, and learn with Paul:

For the love of Christ controls us, having concluded this, that one died for all, therefore all died.
(2 CORINTHIANS 5:14, NASB)

We subconsciously change 'of Christ' to 'for Christ' in this verse. We hear it preached that we ought to love God more, yet this does NOT read love *for* Christ, but rather the love *of* Christ. That is the real, authentic, genuine love of Jesus operating in and through our lives.

When we make this subconscious shift, we actually change something quite supernatural for something small and rather ineffective, which is our own man-made efforts at loving. In fact, as soon as we bring the 'ought to love God more' spirit into our homes, we increase the legalistic pressure and judgemental non-acceptance on all those around us. The very thing we want — the love of Christ — actually starts disappearing and is replaced by our counterfeit version of it. The consequent religious spirit then goes on to destroy many a good home and the relationships within it. Sadly, too many children from these kinds of homes end up leaving church and a spiritual walk as a result. (At least for a season, but grace can reverse even that!)

Thankfully, the verse does not read that it's my love FOR Christ, but His actual love within me that produces change. So, it's not about me loving God more, but letting God's love loose and available within me more. We have to learn how to let the God who lives within us loose.

How do we practically do that? These are some things I have found to be effective.

Practise the Presence of God

As we have already said in this book, it took a while for me to realise that God will never leave me, even on my worst days. He categorically made such a promise. Consequently, I can live with an unending relationship, a continuous conversation. I can bring God into everything, from parking the car to raising the kids. From the difficult student in the classroom to the business deal on the table, God is the expert on it all, and He's ready to advise. David wrote this in the Psalms:

> *But as for me, the nearness of God is my good;*
> *I have made the Lord GOD my refuge,*
> *That I may tell of all Your works*
> (PSALM 73:28, NASB 1995)

Learn How To Hear God

I always find the account in John's Gospel astounding. This is the moment when God speaks from heaven with an audible voice, yet many of those standing there in that moment said the sound was only the sound of thunder (John 12:29). In other words, they did not discern the voice of God. God speaks to us in our spirits, and it's there we learn to hear and recognize His voice. We can discover Isaiah 30:21 to be an everyday reality in our own lives. It says, *Whether you turn to the right or to the left, your ears will hear a voice behind you, saying, "This is the way; walk in it"* (NIV).

In learning how to do this, practise regularly a few spiritual disciplines, including:

- **Reading:** Open your Bible and pray. Before reading, ask God to speak to you from it. Do this often, daily, if possible. We can't say God isn't speaking if our Bibles are shut.

- **Prayer:** Make sure you get moments of stillness without distractions. In our day we often find this one of the hardest things to do. In that stillness, reach out to God. It's often in that still small voice that He speaks.

- **Journaling:** Write down what you think you hear. When you then look back over the things written, you will see a noticeable conversation emerging.

Give God the First Opportunity to Act Through You Before You React to Circumstances

No doubt you will have heard people say to those who tend to lose their tempers, *'Count to ten before you say anything'*. I so often pray many times a day, *'God, please respond through me here'*, or I pray, *'God what is the correct response in this situation?'* It doesn't mean that I always get it right, but it does reduce the number of wrong reactions considerably. It changes the meaning of the word 'responsibility' to '**response-ability**'. God's grace within you increases your response-ability.

Stay in an Attitude of Gratitude

Be grateful for everything God does for you, take nothing for granted. I have learned that if the devil can't stop you from getting a breakthrough, he will stop you from celebrating that breakthrough by keeping you focused on the next problem. Gratitude towards God often leads in then being thankful to others.

Build Up a Reserve of Godly Wisdom

The Bible is full of wisdom for life. Find and learn its principal points, which gives you a head start on grace responses. The book of Proverbs is a great place to start. It's there that we read things like *a gentle answer turns away wrath* (Proverbs 15:1, NASB) or *a man who has friends must himself be friendly* (Proverbs 18:24, NKJV). Practical, workable effective advice then proves yet another Proverb true, *he who wins souls is wise* (Proverbs 11:30, NKJV).

Give Space for Grace

Most times, we never know the story behind the face looking back at us. For many years, we ran a ministry providing a full Christmas dinner on Christmas day for those homeless in our city. We would go out, pick them up and bring them in for a turkey dinner, gifts, fellowship, meeting and some entertainment and fun.

My family and I would often love serving on this day and have our family Christmas dinner the next day. I lost count of the number of times I was astounded to hear the stories of these people, and how they ended up homeless. For most, they didn't run out of money, they ran out of friends.

On one particular Christmas day, out of a crowd of around three hundred homeless people — most of whom did not know each other — I discovered three people who had a PhD, a musician who had played for the prestigious BBC Philharmonic orchestra, a man who had started a well-known business in our area which was still running, and a man who had inherited a million dollars but lost it all through a bad investment.

There were others who had been released from prisons with nowhere to go, the addicts and the mentally sick who had found no place to get help. A musician had nursed his wife through terminal cancer, when she died, he fell apart without her. Unable to cope, he lost everything. The businessman who had been defrauded of his business. There were others who had been abused, hurt and neglected by those who should have looked after them.

Most people with such misfortune don't end up on the streets, but they are found running our cafés and local businesses. We bump into them in the mall. We just don't know the story behind the face. Just as we need all the grace we can get, let's make as much space for the same grace to bring change all around us. When we get a negative or unwelcome response, let's make space for grace, cut some slack, give a listening ear and look for an opportunity to make a difference.

Reach For and Expect the Fruit of the Spirit to Grow in Your Life

Galatians 5:22–23 teaches us about the *fruit* of the Spirit, often confused by some Christians with the gifts of the Spirit. But these are attributes God Himself will produce in our lives as we walk with Him. They include love, peace, patience, kindness and longsuffering. I know that we can pray like the Christian of old '*Lord, give me patience but give it to me quick!*' in those exacerbating moments. But the truth is, God the Holy Spirit is a fruit grower, and the best fruit takes time and attention. All too often we get more concerned with what we must do for God and forget who or what we are becoming in the process.

We as Christian people ought not be static like buildings. We should be changing constantly. Buildings have styles, here in the UK we might say buildings are Victorian or Gothic or maybe Georgian. They were built in that period and stayed in that style. But you and me? The adventure is in the changing, and we can be continuously changing until we reach heaven or Jesus returns. Some people learn all about theology (the study of God) but never get to know the God they are studying. Transformation always leads information as far as God is concerned. We read:

> *But we all, with unveiled face, beholding as in a mirror the glory of the Lord, are being transformed into the same image from glory to glory, just as from the Lord, the Spirit.*
> **(2 CORINTHIANS 3:18, NASB 1995)**

See Yourself as God Sees You

When we hear the often repeated Christian slogan *I am nothing but a sinner saved by grace,* we need to stop and recognize that simply isn't true. It's fake news. The Bible teaches us that the sinner died, he is no more. I am in fact a new creation, called so often in the Bible 'saint'. We may not feel like a saint, we may not always act like a saint, but as far as God is concerned, saints we are. We read:

Therefore, if anyone is in Christ, the new creation
has come: The old has gone, the new is here!
(2 CORINTHIANS 5:17, NIV)

The devil never wants us to see any good thing within our own lives, but only make us mindful of shortcomings and weaknesses. But Paul writing to Philemon, wrote a fantastic thing, he said:

And I pray that the fellowship of your faith may
become effective through the knowledge of every
good thing which is in you for the sake of Christ.
(PHILEMON 1:6, NASB)

Can you see, recognize and identify all that God has given you? Oftentimes others are quicker to see the good things within us than we are ourselves.

Get Into a Real Living Church

Too many give up on church fellowship either because of the difficulties produced with interpersonal relationships, or else it's just no longer convenient.

There are huge benefits to livestreaming and churches online, but not when it comes to a grace filled, grace benefitting life.

You just can't live the life of grace in isolation form others. You haven't been designed that way, and grace hasn't been designed that way. Grace works when grace flows. We are meant to be rivers not swamps. We read:

Real wisdom, God's wisdom, begins with a holy life and is characterized by getting along with others. It is gentle and reasonable, overflowing with mercy and blessings, not hot one day and cold the next, not two-faced. You can develop a healthy, robust community that lives right with God and enjoy its results only if you do the hard work of getting along with each other, treating each other with dignity and honor.

(JAMES 3:17–18, MSG)

I need other people to bring out the best in me, but I also need other people to challenge the worst in me. Only through this interaction and exchange in real life and real-life situations is Christ then formed within you and me. Sometimes enjoyable, often a challenge but always transformational.

Can You Be Kindling?

I asked some young people a few weeks ago if any of them knew what kindling was? They replied, 'It's an eBook reader!' I responded, 'No, that's *Kindle*'. Kindling is an essential product for all good fires.

It's no good trying to light a large log with a match. A hundred boxes of matches would never do it. Those of us used to camp-fires or log fires at home realise we need small bits of dry wood to get the fire started, those small bits of wood are called kindling. Get them going and in no time at all the big logs are blazing.

We often pray 'big log prayers', like *save our city* or *save our nation*, but the truth is God uses kindling. He starts small, with a heart here or a life there. Can He set a fire of love and grace so ablaze in your heart that anyone around you can't help but catch it? Astronomical grace can do that. One single soul, released into immeasurable, undeserved grace can cause its own revival, revolution or reformation.

Paul wrote 14 epistles and every single one of them closes with a prayer for the grace of Jesus to be with them. That is my prayer for you.

Saved by grace alone!
This is all my plea:
Jesus died for all mankind
And Jesus died for me. [41]

NOTES

1   Charles Spurgeon, *Evening by Evening*
    (Abbotsford: Aneko Press, 2020), 229

2   Bono, *Selections from the Book of Psalms: Authorized King James Version*,
    Pocket Canons (New York: Grove Press, 1999) Introduction

3   Thomas Brooks, *Precious Remedies Against Satan's Devices*
    (London: The Religious Tract Society, 1652) 38

4   Charles Spurgeon, *Morning and Evening: Daily Readings* (Grand
    Rapids: Christian Classics Ethereal Library, 1865–1868), 405

5   N.T. Wright, *Jesus and the Victory of God*,
    (London, SPCK Publishing, 2015), 267

6   J.I. Packer, https://www.azquotes.com/quote/863971

7   The New American Standard New Testament Greek Lexicon,
    https://www.biblestudytools.com/lexicons/greek/nas/teleo.html

8   Joshua Nickel, *Walk Between Heaven and Earth: Listening
    to Martin Luther on How to Be a True Theologian*,
    (Kindle, joshuamarknickel.com, 2017)

9   James Strong, *A Concise Dictionary of the Words in the Greek New Testament; with their Renderings in the Authorized English Version,* (New York, Abingdon Press, 1890), 73

10   John Blanchard, *The Complete Gathered Gold,* (Darlington: Evangelical Press, 2006), 14

11   Blanchard, *The Complete Gold,* 1

12   Ibid.

13   Ibid, 371

14   James Strong, *Strong's Greek Dictionary of the Bible* (Nashville: Abingdon Press, 1890), 65

15   René A. Wormser, *The Story of the Law and the Men Who Made It* (New York: Simon and Schuster, 1962), 198

16   John Bunyan, *Grace Abounding to the Chief of Sinners* (London: The Religious Tract Society, 1905), 9–10

17   Joshua Nickel, *Walk Between Heaven and Earth: Listening to Martin Luther on How to Be a True Theologian,* (Kindle, joshuamarknickel.com, 2017)

18   D. Martyn Lloyd-Jones, *Romans: Exposition of Chapter 7:1–8:4,* (East Peoria, Versa Press, Inc., 2010), 277

19   Billy Graham, *https://twitter.com/billygraham/ status/1283435661262049280?lang=cs*

20   Charles Spurgeon, *Morning and Evening: Daily Readings* (Grand Rapids: Christian Classics Ethereal Library, 1865–1868), 451

21   Jim Elliot, *The Shadow of the Almighty* (San Francisco: HarperCollins Publishers, 1979), 93

22 James Strong, *Strong's Greek Dictionary of the Bible* (Nashville: Abingdon Press, 1890), 27

23 Matthew Henry, *The Life of the Rev. Philip Henry, A.M.* (London: J.S. Hughes, 1825), 236

24 Spiros Zodhiates, *The Complete Word Study Dictionary: New Testament*, (Chattanooga, AMG Publishers, 1992), 795

25 Richard Baxter, https://gracequotes.org/author-quote/richard-baxter/

26 W.E. Vine, *New Testament Word Pictures*, (Nashville: Thomas Nelson, 2015), 850

27 John Piper, *Future Grace* (Colorado Springs: Multnomah Press, 2012), 189

28 Matthew Henry, *Commentary on the Whole Bible Volume 1 Genesis to Deuteronomy* (Grand Rapids: Christian Classics Ethereal Library, 2009), 155

29 William Carey, https://www.brainyquote.com/quotes/ william_carey_191985

30 F.B. Meyer *Our Daily Walk* (Zeeland, Reformed Church Publications, 2009), 133

31 Charles Spurgeon, "Observing the King's Word," in *The Metropolitan Tabernacle Pulpit Sermons, Vol. XLIX* (London: Passmore & Alabaster, 1903), 501–502.

32 Charles Spurgeon, *Spurgeon's Sermons on Jesus and the Holy Spirit* (Peabody, Hendrickson Publishers, 2006), 136

33 Tim LaHaye, Jerry B. Jenkins, *Jesus and the Hope of His Coming*, (Eugene, Harvest House Publishers, 2004), 13

34 LaHaye and Jenkins, *Jesus and the Hope of His Coming*, 13

35   Charles Spurgeon, *Collected Works Volume 1*
     (Jasper: Revelation Insight Publishing, 2010), 55–56

36   Joshua Nickel, *Walk Between Heaven and Earth:*
     Listening to Martin Luther on How to Be a True Theologian,
     (Kindle, joshuamarknickel.com, 2017)

37   Alan Redpath, *Victorious Christian Living* (Grand Rapids: Fleming
     H Revel, a division of Baker Book House Company, 1955), 22

38   Redpath, *Victorious Christian Living*, 22

39   Ibid, 21

40   J. Matthew Nance, *Living Wisely,* (Bloomington, WestBow Press, 2018)

41   Kenneth Osbeck, *Amazing Grace: 366 Inspiring Hymn Stories for Daily*
     Devotions, Grace! 'Tis a Charming Sound by Philip Doddridge and
     Augustus Toplady, (Grand Rapids: Kregel Publications, 2002), 165

ABOUT THE AUTHOR

Andrew Owen is the author of several books, the founder of Destiny Ministries, the Senior Pastor at Destiny Church Glasgow, and the Principal of Destiny College.

He oversees a global apostolic network of some 850 churches that have sprung up over the last few years.

The churches are hallmarked by a deep passion for the Word of God, social change and authentic leadership.

He believes that the greatest transforming power on earth is the gospel of Jesus Christ.

Andrew, with his wife Sue, currently present a TV programme that broadcasts across the UK to several million viewers. Andrew and Sue have been married for 40 years at the time of this writing and say that they have been on a God-adventure with their five sons, lovely daughters-in-law, five grandsons, and two granddaughters. They have many personal stories to tell of God's miraculous power at work.

To learn more about Andrew or Destiny Church, visit:
destiny-church.com
destiny-ministries.com
youtube.com/destinychurchonline

Follow Andrew on:

- PastorAndrewOwen
- @andrewdestiny
- @pastorandrewowen